Guiding Readers through Text: A Review of Study Guides

Karen D. Wood
University of North Carolina at Charlotte.

Diane Lapp
San Diego State University

James Flood
San Diego State University

International Reading Association
Newark, Delaware 19714

Director of Publications   Joan M. Irwin
Managing Editor   Romayne McElhaney
Associate Editor   Anne Fullerton
Associate Editor   Karen Goldsmith
Production Department Manager   Iona Sauscermen
Graphic Design Coordinator   Boni Nash
Mechanical Preparation   Cheryl Strum
Design Consultant   Larry Husfelt
Typesetting Systems Analyst   Wendy Mazur
Typesetting   Anette Schütz-Ruff
               Richard James
Proofing   Florence Pratt

Library of Congress Cataloging in Publication Data

Wood, Karen D.
   Guiding readers through text: a review of study guides/Karen D. Wood, Diane Lapp, James Flood.
      p.   cm.
   Includes bibliographical references.
   1. Reading—Aids and devices.   2. Reading comprehension—Aids and devices.   3. Study, Method of.   I. Lapp, Diane.   II. Flood, James.   III. Title.
LC1573.39.W66   1992   92-18588
428.4'071—dc20   CIP
ISBN 0-87207-374-2
Fifth Printing, July 1996

Table of Contents

Foreword

With this publication, Wood, Lapp, and Flood add another useful resource to the professional literature relating to reading instruction. *Guiding Readers through Text* combines a discussion of why and how study guides help students comprehend text with a focus on the most effective ways to use these guides in the classroom.

The authors provide historical context by tracing the development of study guides as an instructional resource. For the bulk of the text, they present an array of study guides, explaining their purposes and illustrating their applications. They end with a set of guidelines that encapsulate the principles governing appropriate and effective use of study guides. Throughout the text, the authors present a balanced perspective on the value of these guides, making clear that they are a powerful resource but not a panacea.

Study guides are instructionally effective when the classroom environment—and the guides themselves—reflect three important conditions:

1. *Content and process have equal importance and are developed simultaneously.* The content emphasized in a guide is dictated by the curriculum-related ideas selected by the teacher as the focus of the lesson. The reading and reasoning processes emphasized are a function of the text for which the guide has been developed. As students use the guide, they develop both an understanding of the content and facility with the processes needed for learning.

2. *Students receive adequate support in the simultaneous learning of content and process.* The metaphor of scaffolding has been widely used in recent literature on instruction. This metaphor is particularly apt in describing the function of study guides. Properly designed, study guides provide support that enables students to deal with increasingly abstract ideas. At the same time, this support helps students apply reading and reasoning processes at more complex levels than they could otherwise.

3. *Guides serve as vehicles for applying the principles of cooperative learning to the study of content-related materials.* Study guides provide a focus for students' cooperative discussions of content-related ideas. They also provide a stimulus for students' cooperative application of appropriate reading and reasoning processes.

This volume makes it possible for classroom teachers to experience immediately the practical value of study guides. In addition, this book provides information that allows teachers to explore the theoretical and philosophical bases for the design and use of study guides. Thus, the authors have provided a volume with double value.

May you read this book with interest and apply its ideas and recommendations with pleasure.

Harold L. Herber
Syracuse University

What Are Study Guides?

Study guides—or reading guides, as they are sometimes called—are teacher-developed devices for helping students understand instructional reading material. Often study guides consist of a series of questions or activities related to the textbook or other material being used in class. Students respond to the questions or engage in the activities as they read portions of text.

This procedure differs in two important respects from the typical practice of asking students to answer the textbook questions at the end of each chapter. First, the teacher has control over the questions in study guides and can thus avoid the pitfalls of commercially developed textbook questions, which often are poorly constructed and require little higher-order thinking on the part of the students. Second, with study guides students don't have to wait until after they're done reading to find out what they are expected to know.

Reading an entire selection or chapter with no assistance can be extremely labor intensive, if not impossible, for some students. Study guides provide assistance without diminishing students' control over their learning; as Wood and Mateja (1983) note, a study guide serves as a "tutor in print form."

Since study guides are designed to accompany reading, not follow it, students know at each section of text which information is important and thus requires more attention and reflection. Page numbers or subheadings are frequently given so students can follow along in the text, alternating reading with responding (see Figure 1).

Figure 1
Study Guide Excerpt

Natural Resources

p. 276	Riches of the Earth	What are our natural resources? Why are they important?
pp. 275-76	Forests	Discuss three facts you have learned from reading this section.
p. 276	Fuels	Look at the graph on this page and find which country produces the most crude oil each year. What do you know about this country?

This example illustrates the basic study guide format, but many other types of guides have been described in the professional literature. Some guides are designed to help students recognize the patterns of text while learning content; other guides teach students how to comprehend ideas imbedded in text at different levels, from explicit to implied; still others require that students take on the point of view of people discussed in the selection. Our purpose in this monograph is to present a comprehensive look at the study guides available. We've provided descriptions and examples of each to help teachers decide which ones to use and when to use them.

Study Guide Effectiveness: Research and Practice

The use of study guides has long been advocated in the professional literature (Durrell, 1956; Earle, 1969; Herber, 1970). Nevertheless, unequivocally supporting research is difficult to come by because of the wide variation in study guides. Herber's work examines the most extensive body of research in this area (e.g., Berget, 1977; Estes, 1969; Maxon, 1979; Riley, 1979). The results of these studies indicate that study guides can be effective aids to comprehension under a variety of circumstances.

Research on the prototype of the study guide—questions interspersed in text—is also extensive, with studies dating back several decades (Distad, 1927; Washburne, 1929). Under the influence of behaviorism, early studies in this area used largely factual, verbatim-level questions (e.g., Frase, 1968a; Hershberger, 1964; Rothkopf, 1972). In contrast, later studies (e.g., Andre et al., 1980; Rickards & DiVesta, 1974), under the influence of cognitive theory, have employed higher-order questions requiring a greater depth of mental processing from the reader. In general, the extensive reviews of research on interspersed questions suggest that such questions tend to improve students' performance on comprehension measures (Faw & Waller, 1976; Frase, 1968b; Rickards & Denner, 1978; Rothkopf, 1972). However, these studies have received much criticism because of their contrived experimental material and preponderance of college-age subjects (MacDonald-Ross, 1978; Rickards, 1979; Tierney & Cunningham, 1984; Wood, 1986). More recent research, conducted in a classroom setting with school-age subjects, has demonstrated that using interspersed questions on a variety of content area textbook selections can significantly improve students' understanding (Wood).

In sum, research and experience show that study guides can help students understand their content area texts by focusing their attention on the major areas of importance within a given chapter or chapter segment. Unfortunately, however, study guides have not always been used effectively in classroom instruction. For that reason, many students have unpleasant memories of this technique. In fact, for some, the thought of completing a study guide is about as attractive as the thought of taking a test. This reaction is not as unreasonable as it may seem. Think about it for a moment: if one is assigned to read a section of text and fill out an accompanying study guide *without receiving any instruction or guidance*, the activity resembles an open-book test. No wonder teachers are skeptical about the educational value of study guides.

This is unfortunate since study guides, when used effectively, do as their name suggests: they guide study before, during, and after a lesson. But to get the most benefit from study guides, teachers must know how to choose (and use) the most appropriate guide for a given learning situation. This book is designed to provide teachers with that knowledge.

Bear in mind that study guides are only a stepping stone to independent learning. Once students have mastered a learning strategy using a study guide, it's important to teach them how to apply that strategy on their own. *A major goal of study guides is to make their use obsolete!*

Types of Study Guides

Numerous variations of study guides are reported in the professional literature. With few exceptions (see Wood, 1988), these guides, although adaptable to elementary levels, were originally designed for secondary students. Given the purposes outlined by the guides' authors, it appears that all study guides are essentially designed to develop two areas: (1) skills and strategies necessary for effective reading, and (2) an understanding of a significant segment of a content area. But while all study guides are similar in intent, they are designed for different classroom contexts, purposes, age groups, levels of independence, and degrees of practice and motivation (Wood, in press).

Figure 2 outlines the various types of study guides described in this book. As you can see, there is a broad array from which to choose. We have provided a brief summary of the primary objectives of each guide to help in your selection. Later sections, which describe each type of guide in detail, provide more specifics about their appropriateness for different class sizes, subject areas, and grade levels. We have found that many guides can be adapted across most or all of these areas. Of course, you should use your own ideas and creativity in modifying them for your students.

After familiarizing yourself with the study guides described later, use this chart to help match your lesson objectives with the most appropriate guide. (The chart provides the page number of each guide's full description.) The next section is designed to help you in this decision-making process.

Figure 2
Types of Study Guides

Primary Objectives and Features	*Guide*	*Page*
Broaden students' perspectives by making use of elaboration and prior knowledge	Point-of-View Guide	11
Help students monitor their comprehension through predicting, retelling, and outlining	Textbook Activity Guide	15
Promote peer interaction through discussion, retelling, brainstorming, and other activities	Interactive Reading Guide	19
Use peer interaction to solidify students' understanding and recall of information heard or viewed	Collaborative Listening-Viewing Guide	23
Help students understand literal, inferential, and evaluative levels of information	Levels-of-Comprehension Guide	27
	Learning-from-Text Guide	31
Enhance students' use of prior knowledge to infer, evaluate, and apply text information through open-ended questions	Guided Learning Plan	35
Activate students' prior knowledge and integrate it with text content; stimulate discussion	Extended Anticipation Guide	39
Teach various processes involved in reading (e.g., drawing conclusions, predicting outcomes, identifying the main idea, sequencing)	Processes-of-Reading Guide	45
Help students understand various organizational patterns of text (e.g., cause/effect, sequencing, comparison and contrast)	Pattern Guide	47
Help students understand the function of main ideas and supporting details through categorization	Concept Guide	51
Extend students' comprehension and recall of main concepts through the use of analogies	Analogical Study Guide	55
Help students develop purposes as they read segments of text; assist students with locating answers and differentiating assignments	Content Guide	59
Help students develop flexibility in reading rate	Guide-O-Rama	61
	Reading Road Map	63
Direct students' attention to text features (figures of speech, concepts, contrasts, main ideas) and help them develop strategies (using context, predicting, drawing conclusions) through the use of marginal notations	Glossing	65
	Process Guide	69

How Do I Choose a Study Guide?

Every teacher has known the frustration of trying to meet the needs of a class full of students with diverse ability levels. In a given heterogenous group, students' reading levels will vary widely. The older the students, the larger the span of differences. For example, a tenth grade classroom may have a ten-year span of achievement that ranges from the fifth grade level to the college level (Singer & Donlan, 1989). In most classrooms, however, a single textbook is assigned for each subject area; all students, regardless of ability level, are expected to read it. Many of these textbooks are what Armbruster (1984) calls "inconsiderate"—that is, they are difficult to understand and assume too much knowledge on the part of the reader. Consequently, it is not surprising that many students have trouble reading and learning from their textbooks.

Study guides can be a great help, but only when chosen and used with care. The following guidelines will help teachers first determine whether a study guide is the most appropriate instructional tool for a given situation, and then decide which one to use.

Decide Whether a Guide Is Needed

Before determining how to teach a particular body of information, you must first decide what you plan to teach about the particular topic. Ask yourself these questions: What concepts do I want my students to know after reading the material? Which vocabulary terms are essential to understanding these concepts? Does the text include important dates, numbers, or other data that students should know? Which subtopics will require more emphasis?

The next step is to determine whether a chapter, a portion of a chapter, or a story warrants the use of a study guide, given the information you want students to learn. Often a teacher will have noted the previous year that the students found one or more chapters of a textbook particularly challenging. They may have been unable to recall or discuss major concepts from those chapters, or their responses may have sounded very literal or "textbook-like," indicating that they had not integrated the new information with their preexisting knowledge. In other instances, the teacher realizes on previewing a text selection that while the content is integral to the lesson objectives, the style, concept load, or mode of presentation is just too overwhelming for independent reading. Help is then needed, particularly for struggling, below-average readers. That help can take the form of a study guide.

It's important to remember that a guide can do only so much. A study guide for a chapter on Japan may focus students' attention on descriptions of topography, industry, people, and other important topics, as well as help them connect that information to their prior knowledge by having them brainstorm what they already know. Yet you may feel that a videotape on the customs of Japan, an outside speaker, or simply more teacher-led discussion would be helpful. In short, do not rely on a study guide as the sole purveyor of content area information. But in combination with your own knowledge, as well as other sources of information, it can be a powerful instructional tool.

Analyze the Material

Once you've determined that a study guide is necessary, the next step is to analyze the material to note its salient features. Is it fiction or nonfiction? Is the primary text pattern cause and effect, main idea and supporting details, or a sequence? Are a lot of related concepts introduced within few pages? Can portions of the selection be skipped? Are the explanations somewhat sketchy and difficult to understand? As you scrutinize the text, these questions and more will begin to surface; their answers will help you decide how the content may best be conveyed.

In concert with this step, you should begin to ask what skills and strategies the reader will need to comprehend the material. Does the text contain gaps that require much inferencing? Is it important that the reader be able to distinguish main ideas from details? Will students benefit particularly from being able to adjust their rate of reading for this selection? Will the students be more motivated to read the selection if they assume the perspective of the main character? Will they learn best by working individually, in small groups, or with the whole class?

Match the Guide to the Material

By now you know what content you want to teach, what the reading material's main features are, and what strategies students will need to understand that material. You also know that a study guide is needed to convey the content effectively. Now it's time to decide which guide best fits your overall lesson objectives.

For this phase in the decision-making process, we will use a specific example. Let's suppose that you are teaching an eighth grade lesson on radioactivity and the next chapter segment deals with detecting radiation. You know that many of your students have had difficulty comprehending the previous chapters, and you decide that giving them some instruction in how to read their science text may help them not only with this chapter but with others as well.

Looking ahead, you see that the next several chapters contain many cause-and-effect passages. Taking this into account along with your lesson objectives, you'd probably select the Processes-of-Reading Guide (described fully later) because it has an extensive modeling component and is thus a good technique for introducing the notion of text structure. Specifically, the Processes-of-Reading Guide takes the students through an entire lesson, beginning with the modeling of the skill or process (e.g., cause and effect, summarizing, sequencing, drawing conclusions, predicting outcomes, locating the main idea) and moving on to examples for whole class use and practice items for small groups or pairs. After working through this initial teaching portion of the guide, students can apply these skills and processes to the textbook selection.

In subsequent reading assignments in science, you can reinforce students' understanding of the cause-and-effect relationship by drawing their attention to relevant patterns of text and eliciting their input. You may also want to describe how this process can be applied in other subject areas.

The Process-of-Reading Guide is well suited to this particular instructional situation and can be adapted to your specific needs. In a different situation—say, if you wanted to focus on the comparison-and-contrast structure—another type of study guide might be more effective. The detailed descriptions that follow should give you the information you need to make the most appropriate choice at any given time.

Point-of-View Guide

In the Point-of-View Guide (Wood, 1988), questions are presented in an interview format to allow students to gain different perspectives on the events described in a reading selection. This format requires students to contribute their own experiences as they assume the role of various characters, thereby enhancing their recall and comprehension.

The purpose of the Point-of-View Guide is threefold. First, it helps develop the important skill of mental elaboration since it requires the students to add their own information as they read. Second, it encourages the skill of mental recitation—the most powerful study technique known to psychologists (Pauk, 1974)—by having students put new information in their own words. Third, it helps students learn the content of the selection.

Since students are unlikely to have encountered this activity before, it will be necessary to model the process thoroughly at the outset. Instruct the students to write their responses in the first person, elaborating whenever possible with information from their experiences. Use examples to show how this type of response differs from typical textbook-like responses. For the text passage that follows, for instance, we've provided a sample question and answer in each style.

> *Text passage:* Even on the battlefield, the lack of American unity was visible. At the Battle of Niagara, a group of New York soldiers, refusing to leave New York, stood and watched their outnumbered comrades across the river being killed.

A point-of-view interview question for this passage might read, "Put yourself in the place of a person living in the U.S. in the early 1800s. In your opinion, were the Americans ready to fight? Explain why you feel this way." A student response might look like this:

> No, we weren't ready to fight. Some of us, the war hawks, wanted war. Others didn't. Some New Yorkers at the Battle of Niagara stood by as their friends got killed. We lacked unity. We didn't even have muskets and other equipment. Some of us had to use our own guns or borrow some.

Note: In this and the following sections, we've provided a breakdown of the group sizes, subject areas, and grade levels for which we think each study guide is best suited. "Classroom context" may be individual, small group, and/or whole class. For our purposes, "Subject" is divided into math, literature, and content areas (e.g., science, social studies). "Levels" are primary (kindergarten to grade 3), intermediate (grades 4 to 5), middle (grades 6 to 8), and secondary (grades 9 to 12).

Classroom Context:
Individual, small group, whole class

Subject:
Literature, content areas

Level:
Primary, intermediate, middle, secondary

The same basic questions—"Was America ready to fight? Why or why not?"—could be found at the end of the textbook chapter. However, in that context they would likely elicit a much different response from students, similar to this one:

> No. Because at the Battle of Niagara, a group of New York soldiers, refusing to leave New York, stood and watched their outnumbered comrades across the river being killed.

In this instance, the student has used the question stem as a starting point and has copied the remainder of the information directly from the text-

Figure 3
Point-of-View Guide
(social studies—intermediate level)

Chapter 11: The War of 1812

You are about to be interviewed as if you were a person living in the United States in the early 1800s. Describe your reactions to each of the events discussed next.

Planting the Seeds of War (p. 285)
1. As a merchant in a coastal town, tell why your business is doing poorly.

The War Debate (pp. 285-87)
2. Explain why you decided to become a war hawk. Who was your leader?
3. Tell why many of your fellow townspeople lowered their flags to half mast. What else did they do?
4. What was the reaction of Great Britain to you and your people at that time?
5. In your opinion, is America ready to fight? Explain why you feel this way.

Perry's Victory (p. 287)
6. In what ways were your predictions either correct or incorrect about Americans' readiness to fight this war?
7. Tell about your experiences under Captain Perry's command.

Death of Tecumseh (p. 288)
8. Mr. Harrison, describe what really happened near the Thames River in Canada.
9. What was Richard Johnson's role in that battle?
10. Now, what are your future plans?

Death of the Creek Confederacy (p. 288)
11. Explain how your people, the Cherokees, actually helped the United States.
12. Tell us about your leader.

British Invasion (pp. 288-90)
13. As a British soldier, what happened when you got to Washington, D.C.?
14. You headed to Fort McHenry after D.C.; what was the outcome?
15. General Jackson, it's your turn. Tell about your army and how you defeated the British in New Orleans.

The Treaty of Ghent (p. 290)
16. We will end our interview with some final observations from the merchant questioned earlier. We will give you some names and people. Tell how they fare now that the war is over: the British, the Indians, the United States, Harrison, Jackson.

From Wood, K.D. (1988). Guiding students through informational text. *The Reading Teacher.* 41(9), 912-920. Reprinted by permission of the International Reading Association.

book. This sort of text-based response typifies the answers often given in a classroom. In contrast, notice how the point-of-view question allows for elaboration, inferential thinking, and speculation. Note also how the interview format frees students to use less stilted, more natural language.

Figure 3 pictures a Point-of-View Guide for an intermediate-level text selection on the War of 1812. To give the students a fuller understanding of events from a variety of perspectives, the guide asks them to take on a number of different roles.

Figure 4 illustrates how this type of guide can be used with a U.S. history lesson at the secondary level. In this case the student assumes the perspective of a person living in the United States after 1941. Question 1 has the students "become" workers in a U.S. defense plant and tell what effect the War Production Board has had on them, their co-workers, and the soldiers overseas. A student's response to this question might read, "Since Roosevelt started up the War Production Board in 1942, we have been busy every minute. We're building twice as many tanks and supplies than ever before. We work like crazy—a lot of overtime, too. The troops overseas ought to be happy though. We're producing more supplies and weapons than all our enemies put together!"

To get the most out of this exercise, students should be encouraged to respond in dialogue whenever possible. Remember that this type of response will require extensive modeling and demonstration.

Figure 4
Point-of-View Guide
(U.S. history—secondary level)

America After 1941

America's Huge War Needs (pp. 617-18)
1. As a worker in a U.S. defense plant, tell what effect the War Production Board has had on you, your co-workers, and the soldiers overseas.

Americans Go Back to Work (p. 618)
2. As one of the leaders in a national labor union, what is your reaction to the need for war supplies?
3. As a farmer, tell how your life has changed from the Depression days to the present days of wartime.

Opportunities for Blacks (pp. 618-19)
As a black person from the south:
4. Tell why you and others moved to the northeast and midwest sections of the U.S.
5. Describe the effect of Hitler's racist doctrine on your situation at home.
6. Tell why Executive Order 8802 was important to you.

The Point-of-View Guide can be used in other subject areas and grade levels as well. In science, for example, students could describe dissection from the perspective of a nematode, photosynthesis from the perspective of a plant, or an eruption from the point of view of a volcano. In a literature class, students can readily assume the roles and emotions of the characters in a selection. One teacher found the point-of-view approach useful in teaching primary students about the meeting of cultures in colonial America. After reading aloud a story about Thanksgiving, the teacher had students write a brief account of their lives as either a pilgrim or a Native American.

Following are some sample point-of-view questions illustrating their application across subject areas.

Science

Text passage: A crocodile can grow to a length of 20 feet, weigh half a ton, and tackle a 900-pound buffalo that wanders past at lunchtime. A crocodile can stay under water for 2 ½ hours without a breath of air by slowing his heartbeat and going into semi-hibernation. He can outrun a man in a 100-yard dash, although there is no record of any such footrace.

Question: Imagine that you are a crocodile swimming down the Zambezi River in Africa. Tell us about yourself and what you are thinking as a tourist wades in the waters nearby.

Language Arts

Text passage: At a little one-room mountain schoolhouse, the big boys in the upper grades enjoyed driving off school teachers. Finally, the school had to close because there was no teacher. A few weeks later, however, a pale, thin, harmless-looking fellow showed up to ask about the teaching job. He was told what he was up against.

Question: You are the teacher who has just shown up for the job. What training have you had? Describe your plans for this class.

Social Studies

Text passage: Britain and France responded to the U.S. trade laws by capturing American merchant ships and seizing their cargoes. Often the British took American sailors and forced them to join the British navy. Although the trade laws hurt France and Britain, they probably hurt the United States more. Shipping businesses in New York, Boston, and other large port cities nearly collapsed.

Question: As a merchant in a coastal town, tell what is happening to your business and why it is doing so poorly.

Textbook Activity Guide

One of the more recent versions of the study guide is Davey's (1986) Textbook Activity Guide, or TAG. TAGs differ from conventional guides in two respects: (1) they require students to work in pairs, and (2) they are based on research in metacognition and therefore have a self-monitoring component.

Included in the TAG is a set of strategy codes directing students to complete one activity for each text portion read; for instance, students may make predictions about a selection, discuss the text with their partner, retell or write a response to information, or draw diagrams or maps. The guide also includes self-monitoring codes that allow students to indicate which portions of the selection need further clarification. Davey's research has shown that TAGs enhance student's overall learning.

The TAG shown in Figure 5 helps students monitor their comprehension by indicating—with a check mark, a question mark, or an x—the degree to which they understand a particular question or segment of text. Strategy codes are explained at the top of the guide and placed beside each question to cue the desired type of response (teachers can change or add strategy codes as needed for a given lesson). Note how Question 1 asks students to survey the text selection with their partners. Surveying a chapter is a good way to "ground" the subsequent reading and to build a framework for connecting new knowledge; including this step on a guide is one way to help students develop this strategy independently.

Developing a TAG involves five steps. Begin by clarifying the lesson objectives for the chapter or text segment under study. Then go through the selection and pick out the headings, portions, and diagrams that relate to your objectives. Next select which text features you want to use in the study guide and sequence them appropriately. The fourth step involves matching the reading/study task to the objective (this is where the strategy codes come in). When the objective calls for inferencing or brainstorming of prior knowledge, the most appropriate task might be to discuss the selection with a partner. When you want students to sequence, organize, or show relationships, having them make a chart or diagram is a logical approach. Choose one task for each text portion on your guide.

The last step in developing a TAG is to create a self-monitoring system that is understandable and helpful to students. Line markers can be placed beside each numbered task for students to indicate their level of understanding. This way, the teacher can walk around the class to see which areas may require additional review or explanation.

Classroom Context:
Small group, whole class

Subject:
Content areas

Level:
Intermediate, middle, secondary

Figure 5
Textbook Activity Guide
(science—middle level)

Fossils

Names_____   Date(s) _____
      _____

Strategy Codes:

  RR – Read and retell in your own words
  DP – Read and discuss with partner
  PP – Predict with partner
  WR – Write a response on your own
  Skim – Read quickly for purpose stated and discuss with partner
  MOC – Organize information with a map, chart, or outline

Self-Monitoring Codes:

  ✓ I understand this information
  ? I'm not sure if I understand.
  X I do not understand and I need to restudy.

1. ___ PP   pp. 385-392. Survey the title, picture, charts, and headings. What do you expect to learn about this section?

2. ___ WR   As you are reading, jot down three or more new words and definitions for your vocabulary collection.

3. ___ RR   pp. 385-86, first three paragraphs.

4. ___ DP   pp. 386-87, next three paragraphs.
             a. Describe several reasons why index or guide fossils are important.
             b. How can finding the right type of fossil help you to identify it?

5. ___ MOC   Map pp. 387-89. Make an outline of the information.

1. _____   2. _____   3._____
   a. _____   a. _____   a._____
   b. _____   b. _____   b._____
   c. _____   c. _____   c._____

6. ___ Skim p. 390, first three paragraphs
             Purpose: To understand the role of the following in the formation of
                      fossils
             ___ a. natural casts
             ___ b. trails and burrows
             ___ c. gastroliths

7. ___ DP   pp. 390-91
             As an amateur fossil collector, describe:
             a. where to find fossils
             b. what to use to find them
             c. how to prepare them for display

8. ___ WR   p. 392, next to last paragraph
             Define pseudofossil. Jot down three other words that contain the
             prefix "pseudo." Use the dictionary if necessary.

9. ___ DP   Examine the fossil collection being passed around and list eight things
             you have learned by analyzing it.

From Wood, K.D. (1987). Helping students comprehend their textbooks. *Middle School Journal.* 18(2), 20-21. Reprinted by permission.

When first implemented, work on the TAG should last approximately one class period; the guide itself should therefore be fairly short. As students gain proficiency in their use, the TAGs can be lengthened and their use can span several class periods.

Since TAGs will probably be new to the students, be certain to explain and demonstrate their use before assigning students to work in pairs. Don't forget to stress why you are using these guides; it is important that students understand the TAG's value as a self-evaluation strategy to enhance their learning.

Interactive Reading Guide

If a major lesson objective is to promote cooperative learning, the Interactive Reading Guide (Wood, 1988) is an appropriate choice. Most study guides were designed for use by students working alone. With the Interactive Reading Guide, the teacher directs the strategy by requiring responses from individuals, pairs, small groups, or the class as a whole. Consequently, unlike most guides, one of this type may take several days to complete. Throughout the lesson, students are asked to make predictions, develop associations, recall what was read (either mentally or in writing), or reorganize information in accordance with the text's structure.

After the students complete each segment, activity, or question, the teacher directs the class in a discussion of the content. The teacher can vary the time spent on each activity as needed. Some segments can be taken slowly, while others may be given a time limit. The more advanced students may be allowed to proceed ahead in certain portions if the teacher so chooses.

Figure 6 depicts an Interactive Reading Guide for an intermediate-level lesson on Japan. Students begin by working in groups to write down everything that comes to mind on the topics listed for Japan. Since these topics were taken directly from the chapter's subheadings, the students can readily match their preexisting knowledge with the the new content they encounter in their reading. After the initial free associating, the guide leads students through a wide variety of activities designed to engage their interest and improve their understanding. The activities range from whisper reading with a partner to putting two pencils together and pretending to eat with chopsticks. Question 6, which asks students to react to a series of statements before and after reading the section on "Industrialized Japan," is a sort of Extended Anticipation Guide (described later in this text). In the final question, the students are to skim over their responses while keeping in mind the topics introduced at the beginning of the guide. A class discussion follows. This review activity serves to reinforce and synthesize the major concepts just learned.

When applied to mathematics, the Interactive Reading Guide helps students see the processes involved in solving word and computation problems (Wood, 1990a). The guide shown in Figure 7 is for an intermediate-level lesson

Figure 6
Interactive Reading Guide
(social studies—intermediate level)

Chapter 12: Japan—An Island Country

Interaction codes:

◯ = Individual

◯◯ = Pairs

◯◯◯ = Group

◯ = Whole class

◯◯◯ 1. In your group, write down everything you can think of relative to the topics listed below on Japan. Your group's association will then be shared with the class.

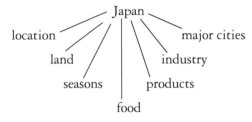

◯
◯◯◯ 2. Read page 156 and jot down 5 things about the topography of Japan. Share this information with your partner.

◯ 3. Read to remember all you can about the "Seasons of Japan." The associations of the class will then be written on the board for discussion.

◯◯ 4. a. Take turns "whisper reading" the three sections under "Feeding the People of Japan." After each section, retell, with the aid of your partner, the information in your own words.

   b. What have you learned about the following?
   terraces, paddies, thresh, other crops, fisheries

◯◯◯ 5. Put two pencils together and allow each person in the group to try eating with chopsticks. Discuss your experiences with the group.

◯◯ 6. With your partner, use your prior knowledge to predict whether the following statements are true or false *before* reading the section on "Industrialized Japan." Return to these statements *after* reading to see if you've changed your view. In all cases, be sure to explain your answers. You do not have to agree with your partner.

   a. Japan does not produce its own raw materials but instead gets them from other countries.

   b. Japan is one of the top 10 shipbuilding countries.

   c. Japan makes more cars than the U.S.

   d. Silk used to be produced by silkworms but now it is a manmade fiber.

   e. Silkworms eat mulberry leaves.

   f. The thread from a single cocoon is 600 feet long.

◯
◯◯◯ 7. After reading, write down 3 new things you learned about the following topics. Compare these responses with those of your group.
        Other industries of Japan
        Old and new ways of living

◯
◯◯◯ 8. Read the section on "Cities of Japan." Each group member is to choose a city, show its location on the map in the textbook, and report on some facts about it.

◯
◯ 9. Return to the major topics introduced in the first activity. Skim over your chapter reading guide responses with these topics in mind. Next, be ready to contribute, along with the class, anything you have learned about these topics.

From Wood, K.D. (1988). Guiding students through informational text. *The Reading Teacher. 41*(9). 912-920. Reprinted by permission of the International Reading Association.

Figure 7
Interactive Reading Guide
(mathematics—intermediate level)

Dividing by Two-Digit Divisors

1. In your groups, work through the sample problem at the top of page 108. Designate one person as the "thinker" to talk through the thinking processes involved and one person as the "writer" to write down the steps. The other members of the group should contribute their thinking, too.

   Hint: The writer can use chart paper so all group members can see the steps.

2. Work through the first two problems in the "Study and Learn" section. Repeat the same procedures as in Question 1, but this time assign different group members the roles of thinker and writer.

3. In pairs, work through the next two problems in the "Study and Learn" section, talking aloud the processes with your partner. Then compare your computations with those of the others in your group. If there is disagreement anywhere in your computations, talk through the processes used.

4. In pairs, work through problems 5 to 12 in the "Divide and Check" section. Compare your computations with those of the rest of your group and discuss any disagreements.

5. Work through the next 10 problems individually. Check and discuss any disagreements with your partner.

6. Talk yourself through and write out the steps for the two word problems in the "Solve Problems" section. Compare answers with the rest of your group and discuss your thinking.

7. With your partner, make up two more word problems that involve dividing by two digits. Work through the answers. Exchange word problems with your group and compare processes.

on "Dividing by Two-Digit Divisors." For illustration purposes, we've made the guide somewhat more verbose than it would normally be. In class, the teacher would include the needed explanation in a demonstration. The teacher should thoroughly model the guide, "walking" students through it step by step. (Research by Good and Grouws, 1979, clearly shows the value of modeling and demonstration in math classes.) Model the "talk aloud" portion by thinking out loud and writing down each procedure one step at a time ("Let's see, first I would see if 22 goes into 11.... Second,...").

The Interactive Reading Guide is a good strategy to use when you've determined that a group of students—or the whole class—needs additional help with a lesson (particularly in math). For management purposes, it is helpful to determine the group assignments before beginning the lesson. That way, the students who will gain most from peer tutoring can be grouped with others who possess more expertise.

Because Interactive Reading Guides require a good deal of oral and graphic response from the students, it may take several days to complete one. The teacher acts as an orchestrator, guiding and directing the students, and as a monitor, overseeing the group interactions and providing help when needed. In the end, the completed guide will give students a synopsis of the textbook content that will be useful for future study and review.

Collaborative Listening-Viewing Guide

The Collaborative Listening-Viewing Guide (Wood, 1990b) is a framework for taking notes from information observed or heard. Teachers can use this type of guide to help them organize the content they want to present. Conversely, students can use it to receive, record, and process the new content with the aid of their peers.

The Collaborative Listening-Viewing Guide has five phases or components: previewing/reviewing, recording, elaborating, synthesizing, and extending information. Working in groups of different sizes, students fill in a form that has spaces for each component. Below we describe these phases before presenting a sample lesson.

Preview/review. As its name implies, this stage can serve two functions. The preview function operates similarly to the "coming attractions" trailers shown in many movie theaters, which provide the audience with a brief overview of an upcoming film. With the Collaborative Listening-Viewing Guide, the preview may consist of a student-directed activity, a teacher-directed activity, or a combination of the two.

A student-directed activity might be a brainstorming session to elicit students' prior knowledge of a particular topic. For example, a teacher may say, "Before we see this videotape on the Industrial Revolution, let's find out what you already know. I'll organize your responses on the board." An activity that involves more teacher direction and less student input might be the presentation of key concepts and vocabulary that will be encountered in the lesson. A lead-in statement for this activity might be, "Our demonstration today will be on static electricity. Since you will hear a few terms that you may not recognize, I'll explain their definitions now and show how each term will be used in the context of the demonstration." The students then write that information in their guides.

The second function of the preview/review phase is to review information already learned from a chapter or unit before introducing a related activity (e.g., a field trip, videotape, or demonstration). The review reinforces the later activity's goal of solidifying and extending the lesson. The teacher directive in this case might be, "We have been studying Greece. Tell me what you remember about Greek customs, old and new, before we meet our guest from Greece."

Classroom Context:
Individual, small group, whole class

Subject:
Math, literature, content areas

Level:
Intermediate, middle, secondary

Record. In the record phase, students are asked to jot down important concepts, phrases, or events as they are listening or viewing. Students should be instructed to keep their notes brief, using abbreviations when possible, so that the transcribing does not interfere with their listening. It is also important that the notes be recorded in sequential order to facilitate the next phase, group elaboration.

Elaborate. In this phase, the students join together in previously established small groups to elaborate on their notes from the record phase. Here they can put their heads together to recall details, flesh out their abbreviated notes, contribute related information, and reorganize the material. This phase should take place as soon as possible after the initial listening/viewing lesson to ensure that the students will be able to remember the significant information.

Synthesize. After the groups have met to elaborate on the initially recorded information, the class as a whole should be consulted to provide yet a broader view on the topic. The teacher may begin this phase by asking, "What are some significant things we have learned from today's observation?" Here is an opportunity to help students make generalizations about the content learned without burdening the discussion with superfluous details. Students can organize and record on their guides the most important concepts contributed by class members.

Extend. The extension phase of the Listening-Viewing Guide allows students to work in pairs to apply the information they've learned. For instance, they may compose a paragraph or two consolidating some of the information, design a project related to the topic, develop a semantic map of the key concepts, write a play or skit, or conduct further research on an aspect of interest to them.

Figure 8 depicts a completed guide for a videotape on oceans. The purpose of the video was to provide students with background information and visual reinforcement for a science unit on oceans. In the preview phase the teacher began by eliciting students' preexisting knowledge of the topic in a brainstorming session and introduced a few interesting facts. The student recorded the relevant information as shown. Although the guide doesn't show it, the teacher also asked students to review the location of the world's oceans by pointing them out on a map.

During the video screening, the student recorded key phrases and terms down the left-hand column of the guide. (What's shown here is an excerpt of those notes.) Afterwards, the students worked in groups to elaborate on each other's notes, trigger new recollections, and consolidate the information. Notice how content missed in the individual notetaking activity was filled in during the elaboration activity (also excerpted here) as the groups pooled their recalled information.

In the synthesis phase, the entire class was asked to brainstorm and contribute concepts they had learned. With the teacher's help, the students then reorganized this information into semantic maps.

Finally, the students were given a variety of options from which to choose for the extension/application phase. The partners for this guide chose to come up with a question to research (and eventually answer) during the rest of the unit on oceans.

Figure 8
Excerpt from a Guide for a Videotape on Oceans
(science—middle level)

Class: *Science*   Topic: *Oceans*

Student's Name: *Kevin*   Other Group Members: *Lauren*

Partner: *Ryan*   *Eric*

Preview/Review: *The world is really one big ocean. 70 percent is water. —not as calm as it looks — always moving. Plants and animals (some weigh tons and some can't be seen) can change salt water to fresh water. Ocean bottom is six miles below surface (from our school to fairgrounds). Atlantic, Pacific, Indian, Arctic, Antarctic.*

Record (individually)	Elaborate (groups)
World oceans — Pacific is largest	*Pacific, Atlantic, and Indian in order of size make up World oceans — also Artic and Antarctic*
ocean scientists	*Oceanographers are scientists who study the sea.*
swimming easier	*Swimming is easier because salt helps us float — contains common table salt.*
Blue whales	*Ocean is home to largest animals that ever lived. Blue whales can be 95 ft. Smallest is only 1/25,000 of an inch.*
three types of life: nekton, plankton (jellyfish, small drifting)	*Nekton — can swim around like fish, squid, whales, seals. Barracuda can swim at 30 mph. Many fish can't live everywhere in ocean because of temperature and food supply. Plankton — floating, drifting plants and animals (jellyfish). Benthos — plants and animals that live on the bottom of the ocean — sponges, starfish, coral, and oysters — fixed to bottom and can't move.*

Figure 8
(continued)

Synthesize (whole class)
_____

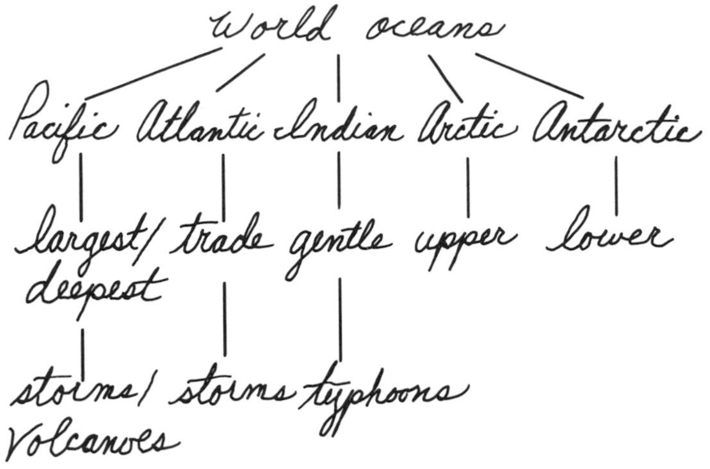

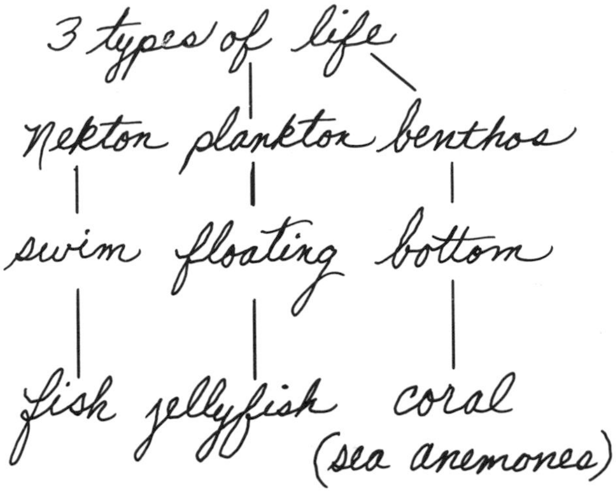

World oceans

Pacific Atlantic Indian Arctic Antarctic

largest/   trade gentle upper lower
deepest

storms/   storms typhoons
Volcanoes

3 types of life

nekton plankton benthos

swim   floating   bottom

fish jellyfish   coral
                (sea anemones)

Extend/Apply (pairs)
_____

Our study question for this unit is: How old is the ocean
and how did oceans begin?

_____

From Wood, K.D. (1990). The collaborative listening-viewing guide: An aid for notetaking. *Middle School Journal, 22*(1), 53-56. Reprinted by permission.

Levels-of-Comprehension Guide

Frequently cited in the literature on secondary school learning is Herber's (1970) Levels-of-Comprehension (or Three-Level) Study Guide. Herber believes that reading comprehension can be simplified by defining it as a three-level process involving literal, interpretive, and applied comprehension. One of the guide's major purposes is to make students aware of these levels and the differences among them. By leading students through the three-level process, the guide lets them experience what it is like to comprehend at each level.

To achieve these ends, the Levels-of-Comprehension Guide uses declarative statements instead of questions. Students must determine the appropriateness and logic of each statement and find support for their answers in the text passage.

To show how this idea can be applied in middle-level classrooms, we have developed a guide for a science lesson on food chains and food webs (Figure 9). In each section, students are instructed to find evidence in the text that supports their answer. Question 3 under the third level is an example of how a common idiomatic expression (the early bird gets the worm) can be tied in to a content area lesson. Students must engage in higher order thinking to draw analogies between this expression and the content of the lesson. A student might support the view that this expression is based (at least in part) on scientific truth by saying, "The food chain shows how important being a survivor (in many cases an aggressive survivor) is to all living things. For example, if a mouse did not actively seek grain, it might die and would be one less food or energy source for the owl who depends on mice for food."

In Figure 10 we show how the Levels-of-Comprehension Guide can be used in a secondary-level English class which, in this case, is studying John Steinbeck's *The Pearl*. The guide clearly leads students from a lower (literal) level to a higher level of abstraction via the use of strategically developed statements.

Classroom Context:
Individual, small group, whole class

Subject:
Math, literature, content areas

Level:
Intermediate, middle, secondary

▼ ▼ ▼

Figure 9
Levels-of-Comprehension Guide
(science—middle level)

Food Chains and Food Webs

I. *Literal Level*

As you read "Food Chains and Food Webs," decide which of the statements below are clearly stated in the text. Mark each statement that is clearly stated in the text and be prepared to support your choices.

_____ 1. When a mouse eats a grain, energy is passed from the grain to the mouse.

_____ 2. A food chain is the transfer of energy, in food form, from one organism to another.

_____ 3. The sun is an important source of light.

II. *Interpretive Level*

Read the following statements. Mark each statement that expresses an idea that can be supported with information in the text section you have just read. Be prepared to discuss the supporting evidence.

_____ 1. Owls eat mice, snakes, and rabbits; this makes them all part of a food web.

_____ 2. Only some consumers are part of a food web.

_____ 3. When mice eat grain, they are receiving energy from the sun.

III. *Applied Level*

Read the following statements. Mark each statement that you think is reasonable and that can be supported with information from the text combined with what you already know.

_____ 1. Humans are major consumers in a food chain.

_____ 2. We could live without energy from the sun.

_____ 3. The early bird gets the worm.

Note how students' responses change at each successive level in the examples that follow (drawn from the guide in Figure 10).

I. Literal Level

3. Kino and Juana's baby, Coyotito, was stung by a scorpion.

Student response: On p. 617 it says the scorpion landed on the baby and struck.

II. Interpretive Level

4. When Kino learned they could not see the doctor, he became very angry.

Student response: At the end of the chapter, when Kino learns the doctor will not see him, he hits the gate so hard with his fist that his knuckles bleed.

III. Applied Level

    1. We judge others by the clothes they wear.

    Student response: Kids at school judge each other by the way they dress. Adults do it, too. In the story, the people from the town looked at the way Juana and Kino were dressed and decided they were poor.

An interesting adaptation of the Levels-of-Comprehension Guide is described by Vacca and Vacca (1989). In their guide, the levels correspond with Raphael's (1984) notion of question-answer relationships (QARs), which classifies questions on the basis of where the answer can be found—on the page, in the readers' head, or a combination of both.

Figure 10
Levels-of-Comprehension Guide
(English—secondary level)

The Pearl, by John Steinbeck

I. *Literal Level*
As you read Chapter 1 of *The Pearl,* decide which of the statements below are clearly stated in the chapter. Mark those that are clearly stated and be prepared to support your choices.

_____ 1. As Kino awoke in the early morning, he could hear waves splashing on the beach.

_____ 2. Kino heard music playing somewhere as he awoke.

_____ 3. Kino and Juana's baby, Coyotito, was stung by a scorpion.

_____ 4. The neighbors came when they heard the baby screaming.

_____ 5. When Kino and Juana took Coyotito to the doctor, they were told that the doctor would not see them.

II. *Interpretive Level*
Read the following statements. Mark each statement that expresses an idea that can be supported with information from Chapter 1 of *The Pearl.* Be prepared to discuss the supporting evidence.

_____ 1. Kino and his family were well off by the standards of their village.

_____ 2. Juana was superstitious although she believed in God.

_____ 3. In Kino's village, it was almost unheard of for anyone to seek help from the doctor.

_____ 4. When Kino learned they could not see the doctor, he became very angry.

_____ 5. Kino's neighbors were indifferent to his problems.

III. *Applied Level*
Read the following statements. Mark each statement that you think is reasonable and that can be supported with information from the text *combined* with what you already know.

_____ 1. We judge others by the clothes they wear.

_____ 2. The poor are regularly discriminated against.

_____ 3. Medicine is a noble profession and doctors are all noble people.

The guide shown in Figure 11, developed for a middle-level remedial math class, follows this format. The Level I statements are explicitly stated in the text and can be found right on the page. This part of the guide asks students to demonstrate what the textbook explicitly taught them. The Level II statements require that students think and search using both what they learned from their textbook and what they already know. Students can find Level III answers on their own. These answers require students to use their own knowledge to synthesize, extend, and apply the new information to other situations.

Figure 11
Levels-of-Comprehension Guide
(mathematics—middle level)

Fractions

I. *Right There:* What did the material say?
Directions: Check each statement below that you can find on the pages you just read.

____ 1. 49/52 is a fraction.

____ 2. A fraction has two numbers.

____ 3. A fraction is a whole of a part.

____ 4. 50¢ = half a dollar.

____ 5. Fraction = $\dfrac{\text{parts used}}{\text{total parts}}$

____ 6. You must use two numbers to write a fraction.

II. *Think and Search:* What does the material mean?
Directions: Check each statement below that you think is true and can defend.

____ 1. Fractions are important in your life.

____ 2. You can make a fraction by putting the number 3 inside the circle: $\dfrac{\bigcirc}{4}$

____ 3. You can make a fraction by putting the number 8 inside the circle: $\dfrac{\bigcirc}{8}$

____ 4. 3/5 means ●●●○○.

III. *On Your Own:* How can you use fractions?
Directions: Check each item you agree with.

____ 1. You are on an elevator with seven persons. Two out of the seven are men; 2/7 of the people are men.

____ 2. Start with 8. Take half of it. Take half of the answer, then half of the last answer. Keep on doing this. Pretty soon you will reach zero (0).

____ 3. Pete Rose had three hits in five at-bats. You can say this by writing a fraction.

Excerpted from *Content Area Reading*, 3rd ed., by Richard T. Vacca and Jo Anne L. Vacca (p. 173). Copyright ©1989, 1986 by Richard T. Vacca and Jo Anne L. Vacca. Reprinted by permission of HarperCollins publishers.

Learning-from-Text Guide

Singer and Donlan (1980) state that reading objectives can be divided into two types: cognitive and affective. Underlying this notion is their belief that mastery of objectives at lower levels is necessary for mastery of objectives at higher levels. Therefore, in the Learning-from-Text Guide, the authors suggest that teachers analyze the relevant content and break it down into these three levels: (1) information that is explicit or directly stated, (2) information that reflects significant relationships, inferences, and interpretations, and (3) information that lends itself to generalizations and evaluations. While the first two levels are concerned largely with cognitive objectives, the third level can be used to elicit students' affective and critical responses with question stems such as, "How did you feel about...."

The Learning-from-Text Guide is similar to Herber's (1970) Levels-of-Comprehension Guide in that both lead the learner through the literal, explicit level of information to the inferential level and finally to the evaluative or applied level. The major difference between the two guides is that Herber recommends responding to statements, whereas Singer and Donlan's original guide has students answer questions. In a more recent edition of their book, however, Singer and Donlan (1989) show guides that use statements, which they say are better for fostering inquiry and open discussion.

Singer and Donlan (1989) recommend using the following steps in constructing a Learning-from-Text Guide:

Step 1   Read the selection to determine the important content, remembering that students need not always be responsible for learning all of the information presented.

Step 2   Categorize the important content according to the three levels of information. It's usually easier to work backwards—that is, start by constructing generalized or evaluative questions or statements, then decide on the inferences and interpretations that support them, and finally list the explicit information that supports the inferences and generalizations.

Step 3   For the explicit, factual level of the guide, intersperse statements that appear in the text with a few that don't. The stu-

Classroom Context:
Individual, small group, whole class

Subject:
Math, literature, content areas

Level:
Primary, intermediate, middle, secondary

dents must differentiate between the two by writing down the page numbers for statements that come from the text. If you use questions instead of statements, you can indicate the page number on which the answer appears.

Step 4 To construct the inferential level of the guide, it's important to develop questions or statements that will help students (1) perceive the relationships among sentences, and (2) infer or interpret information to arrive at a conclusion. An example follows:

Text passage: The soldiers settled into the trenches and waited for a signal.

Question: For what possible signals were the soldiers waiting?

Statement: During wartime, soldiers must pay attention to many signals.

The students may infer that the soldiers were waiting for an offensive move from the enemy or a sign from their officer before opening fire. The term "trenches" suggests that the soldiers were getting ready to fight, if necessary. That, along with the phrase "settled into," tends to remove the possibility that the signal might be to disperse and relax fire.

Step 5 Like the inferential level, the generalization or evaluative level of the guide can be constructed using either questions or statements. An example of each for the previous text passage might be:

Statement: During wartime, soldiers are always on edge.

Question: How do you think a soldier must feel while waiting in the trenches?

The statement allows the reader to offer the possibility that not all soldiers would be on edge (if, for example, they were not on the front lines) or that the human body cannot stay on edge constantly and must release the tension at some time. The question can elicit an even more personal response from students becaue it asks them to put themselves in the position of a soldier during wartime.

To broaden their thinking, students can work in pairs or small groups to brainstorm and exchange possible answers. These affective responses can be put into written form as well.

We have adapted the Learning-from-Text Guide for an intermediate-level science lesson (Figure 12). In this example, students are instructed to work in pairs to answer the questions listed. They begin by working through questions at the literal level; the guide provides an information index to help them locate the page and paragraph in the text where the answer can be found. Next, students answer questions at the inferential level to help them read between the lines and merge the text-based information with their background knowledge. Finally, they extend this newly learned content to a higher level of generalization by drawing a connection between the text information and their own beliefs about recycling.

Figure 12
Learning-from-Text Guide
(science—intermediate level)

Using Rocks and Soil

As you read pages 198-201, "How People Use Rocks and Soil," answer the following questions with your partner.

A. *Literal Level*
   1. What do we call rocks that have large amounts of useful minerals? (p. 198, paragraph 3)
   2. Name three things made from the mineral copper. (p. 198, paragraph 3)
   3. Name two places ores are found. (p. 199, paragraph 2)
   4. What is a natural resource? (p. 200, paragraph 1)
   5. When materials can be used over and over again, we say they can be
      _____. (p. 200, paragraph 2)
   6. What can add nutrients to soil? (p. 201, paragraph 1)

B. *Inferential Level*
   1. How are rocks important to people?
   2. Why is it important not to waste mineral resources?
   3. Why must open-pit mines be filled in after the ore is mined?

C. *Generalization or Evaluative Level*
   1. In your opinion, what is the value of recycling items?
   2. If you wanted to start a recycling program in your community, what things would you collect to be recycled?

Guided Learning Plan

Like traditional study guides, Guided Learning Plans (GLPs) (Lapp & Flood, 1991) guide or direct the reader purposefully through the text. They differ from most traditional guides in two ways: (1) they actively involve students through open-ended questions that ask them to infer, evaluate, and apply information to new situations; and (2) they prompt students to respond personally to information in the text, thereby integrating it with their prior knowledge.

GLPs should begin with questions that ask for explicit information so students will develop a knowledge base for comprehending the text's content. It is important to let students know that the guide's purpose is to help them better understand and remember what they read. Let them know that completing the guide will make their learning easier and more complete. Typical directions for a Guided Learning Plan might look like this:

> Directions: As you read the text, complete the following study guide.
> Turn to the guide after reading each section.

The Guided Learning Plan in Figure 13 was developed to accompany a filmstrip about King Tutankhamen. Notice that the GLP begins with explicit questions, and that interspersed with questions about the Egyptian king are questions about California (the state in which the GLP was used) and the United States. By mixing questions related to the filmstrip with questions about familiar territory, the teacher allows students to apply what they already know to the new information. Also, notice that the open-ended question at the end is designed to elicit students' personal responses to the material.

Our next GLP example relates to a text chapter about birds (Figure 14). As with the previous guides, this one begins by simply asking for information from the text. It then moves quickly to questions that elicit students' personal responses based on their prior knowledge and experiences. Students are also required to apply what they have learned to new situations, as in Question 5, which asks students to relate their knowledge of birds to airplane design. In addition, several questions ask students to compare and contrast ideas presented in the text.

Guided Learning Plans are especially useful as study guides because they address the complex processes associated with learning from reading. They guide students not only to look for specific information, but also to link their prior knowledge with information in the text and to think critically about the ideas presented (e.g., by applying, comparing, contrasting, or evaluating).

Classroom Context:
Individual, small group, whole class

Subject:
Content areas

Level:
Intermediate, middle, secondary

Notice that page numbers are included in this example to help students find the appropriate segment of the text. Since many content area chapters are laden with unfamiliar concepts and vocabulary, we believe that it is important to guide students to the significant information so they can think about what it means rather than about where it's located. Remember that this is not a test; rather, it is an attempt to guide study/learning time.

Figure 13
Guided Learning Plan
(social studies—intermediate level)

Treasure of the Boy King Tut: Filmstrip study sheet #1

1. What is an obelisk?_____
_____

2. What is the capital city of Egypt?_____
What is the capital city of California?_____

3. Is the capital of Egypt a small, rural city or a crowded, modern city?_____
_____
How does this city compare with the capital of California?_____
_____

4. In the capital of Egypt, do merchants sell most of their goods in shops or on the street?_____
How do these merchants compare with San Diego merchants?_____
_____

5. What is the primary river of Egypt?_____
What are the primary or major rivers of the United States?_____
_____

6. What is the land around Egypt's primary river like, and what is this land used for?
_____

7. As one moves away from the river, what is the land like?_____
_____

8. Why did the ancient Egyptians bury their pharaohs in pyramids?_____
_____

9. What were some of the objects that were buried in the tombs?_____
_____

10. What would you do if you found some of these objects?_____
_____
_____
_____

Figure 14
Guided Learning Plan
(science—middle level)

Birds

1. Why is it that you and many other mammals and birds don't have to hibernate during the winter? (p. 213)

2. What is the advantage of maintaining a constant body temperature? (p. 214)

3. In cold weather, how do you stay warm? What similar method does a bird use to stay warm? (p. 214)

4. Why is it not a compliment when someone tells you that you "eat like a bird"? (p. 214)

5. If you were an airplane designer, what bird characteristics would you wish to imitate in your design? (p. 215)

6. How do birds avoid getting out of breath while flying? Why can't you do this when you're running or walking quickly? (p. 215)

7. Compare the bird's heart to that of an amphibian. Does a bird's heart function like yours? Explain. (p. 201, 215)

8. Can all birds fly? Give reasons and examples for your answer. (p. 215)

9. Describe some of the advantages birds derive from their plumage. (pp. 214-16)

10. How would you dress if you wanted to avoid attracting attention? If you wanted to attract someone? Explain how your answer relates to birds' plumage. (p. 216)

11. How do birds fertilize their eggs? (p. 216)

Figure 14
(continued)

12. Why do most birds take care of their young? Is this similar to the reasons humans take care of their young? (p. 216)

13. Why is a duck's foot shaped differently from a hawk's foot?

14. What are some of the different functions of birds' beaks? (p. 216)

15. Name two ways that birds are helpful to humans. (p. 217)

16. Name three ways in which birds can be harmful to humans. (p. 217)

17. What are some of the common misconceptions you've heard about birds?

18. Would you like to be a bird? Explain why or why not.

Extended Anticipation Guide

The idea of presenting a series of statements to guide students' responses before, during, and after reading a selection has been discussed extensively in the professional literature on content area instruction. Among the first to use such statements was Herber (1970), who included them in his Reasoning Guide, a teacher-developed strategy for eliciting analytical thinking and discussion about topics under study. Readence, Bean, and Baldwin (1981) describe the Anticipation (or Reaction) Guide and Nichols (1983) the Prediction Guide, which are similar in purpose and format in that they use carefully designed statements to stimulate thinking and activate prior knowledge.

More recently, Duffelmeyer, Baum, and Merkley (1987) modified this notion with the Extended Anticipation Guide. The major difference between the original Anticipation Guide and the modification by Duffelmeyer and his colleagues is that the latter demands more active student involvement during the independent reading stage and therefore more closely resembles a study guide.

The teacher begins by introducing the guide before reading as a means of stimulating discussion and finding out what students already know about a topic. The first part of the guide lists statements about the subject discussed in the text and asks students to indicate whether they agree or disagree (see Figure 15). Next, students are instructed to read the selection, using the statements in Part 1 to guide their reading. If desired, they can make mental or written notes of related content as they read.

In Part 2 of the guide, students must find support in the text for their responses in Part 1. If no support is found in the text, students rewrite in their own words what the selection does say about that concept.

From our experiences in demonstrating the Extended Anticipation Guide in classrooms, we've learned that it is best to preassign students to pairs or small groups to complete the guides (Figure 16). Students can take turns reading each of the statements aloud and then share their reactions by agreeing or disagreeing with them. They must substantiate their responses by citing one or more reasons, examples, hypotheses, or anecdotes. Without this all-important substantiation step, the task resembles a true-false exercise devoid of the rich discussion and elaboration that can ensue.

Classroom Context:
Individual, small group, whole class

Subject:
Math, literature, content areas

Level:
Primary, intermediate, middle, secondary

Figure 15
Extended Anticipation Guide
(science—middle level)

Directions: Read each statement in Part 1. If you believe that a statement is *true,* place a check in the Agree column. If you believe that a statement is *false,* place a check in the Disagree column. Be ready to explain your choices.

Part 1

Agree	Disagree	
✓	___	1. Worms die when they are cut in half.
✓	___	2. Some living things don't need sunlight.
___	✓	3. Some animals can grow a new body part after it has been cut off.
___	___	4. Animals that don't have noses can't smell.
___	___	5. Laying eggs and giving live birth are the only ways that animals can reproduce.
___	___	6. All worms have round bodies.

Directions: Now you will read information related to each of the statements in Part 1. If the information you read supports your choices above, place a check in the Support column in Part 2. If the information does *not* support your choices above, place a check in the No Support column and write what the selection says in your own words.

Part 2

	Support	No Support	In Your Own Words
1.	___	✓	Some flatworms split apart and become two flatworms.
2.	✓	___	
3.	___	✓	If you cut off a flatworm's head, it will grow a new one.
4.	___	___	
5.	___	___	
6.	___	___	

From Duffelmeyer, F.A., Baum, D.D., & Merkley, D.J. (1987). Maximizing reader-text confrontation with an Extended Anticipation Guide. *Journal of Reading, 31,* 146-150. Reprinted with permission of Frederick A. Duffelmeyer and the International Reading Association.

Figure 16
Extended Anticipation Guide for Partners or Small Groups
(literature—intermediate level)

Directions: Take turns reading each statement in Part 1 with your partner. If you believe the statement is *true*, put a check in the Agree column. If you believe it is *false*, check the Disagree column. Be ready to explain your answer to each other and the class.

Part 1

Agree	Disagree	
✓	___	1. Superintendents are the people who run schools.
✓	___	2. It is boring to do the same thing every day.
___	✓	3. Sometimes doing the same thing and hearing the same sounds makes you feel comfortable.
___	✓	4. People who live alone don't really need other people.
✓	___	5. People depend on each other a lot.

Directions: You will read about information related to each of the statements in Part 1. If the information supports your previous choice, put a check in the Support column in Part 2. Use the In Your Own Words column to add any additional details from the selection read. If the information does not support your choice, put a check in the No Support column and write what the selection does say in your own words.

Part 2

Support	No Support	In Your Own Words
___	✓	1. They can also take care of apartment buildings.
✓	___	2. Yes, everybody needs a change — even Maxie.
✓	___	3. Even the milkman counted on Maxie to put out her cat on time. This helped him know he was on schedule.
___	✓	4. Maxie was unhappy and really needed friends.
✓	___	5. The people in the story depended on each other to make sure they were on time.

It is also important to establish a relaxed and comfortable environment in which students are free to risk their own opinions. Many students are unaccustomed to responding to open-ended statements; they are more familiar with questions for which there is a single correct answer. With this activity, they should be encouraged to make educated guesses based on their prior knowledge.

A student exchange after reading the first statement in Part 1 of Figure 16 ("Superintendents are the people who run schools") might sound like this:

> Student A—That's right. Just like Ms. Ramirez, superintendent of our school system.
>
> Student B—Yeah, you're right. I'm going to put a checkmark on the agree side.
>
> Student C—I don't know. We used to live in an apartment building and the guy who ran it, Mr. Casey, was called the superintendent. One time when we had a leaky faucet, he came in and fixed it.

In this case, the students are hypothesizing about the meaning of a word. Students should always feel free to disagree with their partners. It is through shared experience that students' views of the world become broadened.

Part 2 of the guide is also most useful if done in pairs or small groups. Students then have the chance to share what they recall about the selection. After reading the story "Maxie," for instance, students would have discovered that there are indeed two meanings for the word superintendent (as offered by Student C in the preceding example). With the statements as their guides, they have the opportunity to make this discovery on their own, as active readers, without being asked to look up the word in the dictionary before reading.

Asking students to respond to a series of statements need not be restricted to science, social studies, and literature classes; it can be applied to mathematics as well (Wood, 1990a). In Figure 17 we show how the concept of the Extended Anticipation Guide (called a Reaction Guide here) can be used after a lesson or unit to solidify students' understanding of important concepts.

In this case, the guide contains some deliberately incorrect statements. For example, Question 2 reflects a common student misconception that the last digit determines the relative size of a number. Encountering the misconception in written form helps students think aloud with their peers and find evidence in their text, their notes, or their own knowledge for their responses. Encourage students to be anecdotal whenever possible to help them relate math problems to everyday life. The last two responses illustrate how students can use information from varied sources to justify their reactions.

One of the greatest assets of the Extended Anticipation Guide is that it gives teachers the opportunity to witness cognitive growth. They see where students are in their thinking in the prereading stage and they get to eavesdrop on students' new learning, as reflected in discussions, during the postreading stage.

Figure 17
Reaction Guide
(mathematics—intermediate level)

Directions: With your partner or in your group, take turns reading and discussing each of the statements below. Check whether you agree or disagree with each statement. Be sure to support your answer with at least one example. Use your book or any other sources for support.

1. When comparing numbers, always start with the digits at the far left.

   I agree ✓   I disagree _____   because: *If you look at the right side your answer could be wrong. We learned that at the beginning of p. 37. The example showed that 42 is greater than 38 even though 2 is less than 8.*

2. 229 is greater than 231 because 9 is greater than 1.

   I agree _____   I disagree ✓   because: *Even though the last number is bigger in 229, you have to look at all three numbers together to really know.*

3. Digits in the tens place are more important than digits in the ones place when comparing numbers.

   I agree ✓   I disagree _____   because: *Numbers in the tens place make the whole number bigger.*

4. 229 < 231

   I agree ✓   I disagree _____   because: *Even though the 9 is bigger than the 1, it is still less. The example on p. 72 of our book says look in the first column, then the second.*

5. Comparing numbers is useful only in math class.

   I agree _____   I disagree ✓   because: *We compare numbers with sports scores, test grades, sizes of things, using recipes and lots of things. We even compared numbers in gym class Tuesday when we got measured.*

Processes-of-Reading Guide

Singer and Donlan (1980) maintain that the various processes involved in reading can be taught with a guide. Their Processes-of-Reading Guide focuses on one skill or process (e.g., determining cause and effect, sequencing, drawing conclusions, predicting outcomes, summarizing, locating the main idea) as it relates to a content area lesson. The guide begins by modeling the skill before moving on to examples for whole class use and practice items for small groups or pairs. After working through the initial teaching portion of the guide, students are referred to the textbook selection to apply the skill or process being taught.

The guide shown in Figure 18 begins with a realistic, everyday example of cause and effect. We have found that the best initial strategy is to present an example of an everyday event to the class and then "think aloud" one or more possible causes. After selecting a cause, use the same procedure to come up with a possible effect. This strategy models the thinking processes involved in comprehending. For the next three everyday examples, you can enlist the aid of the class as a whole in thinking aloud some possible causes and effects.

Once you're comfortable that the students understand the skill being emphasized, move to Part 2 of the guide, which directs students to apply the skill to their subject matter lesson. Rather than sending the students into the text unaided, you may elect to work through one or more items in this section by talking about possible responses and having the class find support in the text. Then students can read the text selections individually and pair up with a partner to complete the rest of the guide. Sharing their thinking with a peer this way will help students strengthen their learning. After the students have completed the application phase of the guide, you can reinforce the lesson by engaging them in a class discussion of their responses.

Classroom Context:
Individual, small group, whole class

Subject:
Content areas

Level:
Intermediate, middle, secondary

▼ ▼ ▼

Figure 18
Processes-of-Reading Guide
(history—middle level)

Cause and Effect

I. Just knowing the order in which events happen is not enough. In reading and understanding history it is impor-
    tant to know the causes and effects of the events. Try to figure out what caused these events and what the effects of
    the events were.

Example
Tim skinned his knee.
    Cause: He fell off his bike when it hit a rut in the road.
    Effect: Tim will need to wash the wound and may need a bandage.

1. Scott got a D in social studies on his report card.
    Cause: He didn't study.

    Effect: His parents will make him study social studies every day.

2. Your older sister runs out of gas on the way to pick you up after your music lesson.
    Cause: She forgot to check the gas gauge.

    Effect: She'll have to get someone to help her get gas.
    She'll be very late picking you up.

3. Christopher Columbus landed in the Americas.
    Cause: He was looking for trade routes to the Orient.

    Effect: It opened a whole new world to the Europeans.

II. Now relate cause and effect to our history lesson: Read "The Industrial Revolution" on pages 178-81.

    As you read pages 178-79, jot down the causes of the following:

1. Between 1760 and 1840 cities in England grew faster than ever before.
    a. Factories were built in cities.

    b. People began to move to cities to work in the factories.

2. The flying shuttle and spinning jenny were invented.
    a. Textile production was slow.

    b. The growing population demanded more cloth.

    As you read pages 179-81, jot down the effects of the following:

1. Steam-powered factories were built all over England during the 1800s.
    a. More people came to towns.

    b. Other countries began to build factories.

    c. 1800s— Factories for producing many things other than textiles
        began to be built.

2. The first electricity generating plant was built in England in 1881.
    a. Electricity could be used to power factory machines.

    b. More inventions were possible.

Pattern Guide

The primary purpose of the Pattern Guide as described by Herber (1970) and Vacca (1981) is to help students become sensitive to the various ways textbook selections can be organized (e.g., cause and effect, comparison and contrast, sequence, enumeration). This guide is developed to coordinate with the predominant pattern in a given text. The assumption underlying the Pattern Guide is that the ability to perceive text organization is a highly sophisticated skill that most readers do not develop independently. A Pattern Guide scrambles the text's organization and requires the students to piece it back together in a logical order. To do so, they must examine and think about the relationships that exist within a given pattern.

Pattern Guides can take any of a number of forms, depending on the subject and on the learning level of the students. The basic procedure remains the same, however. Following is a modified version of the teaching sequence recommended by Vacca (1981) and Herber (1970):

Step 1 Begin by examining the text selection to determine the most prevalent pattern. Keep in mind that (1) patterns of text can vary throughout a book, and (2) students are frequently unable to determine these patterns without ample teacher guidance.

Step 2 Explain to students that their content area books contain various text patterns and that recognizing and using these patterns can further their understanding of the material.

Step 3 Model the text pattern under study by using everyday examples before asking students to transfer their knowledge to their reading assignment. For example, if you're discussing the comparison and contrast pattern, you may want to alert students to words that signal this pattern (see Figure 19).

Next, demonstrate how these signal words are used in everyday speaking and reading to indicate that items, events, or people are being compared or contrasted. Consider this example from a newspaper article: "While some people supported the governor's position on an increased sales tax, a much greater number indicated extreme displeasure by protesting at the state capitol." Here, the use of the word "while" sets the reader up to expect contrasting ideas.

Classroom Context:
Individual, small group, whole class

Subject:
Content areas

Level:
Primary, intermediate, middle, secondary

▼ ▼ ▼

Step 4 Be certain that whole class and small group discussion is used frequently throughout the lesson to further solidify understanding and to correct possible misconceptions.

Figure 19
Text Pattern Signals

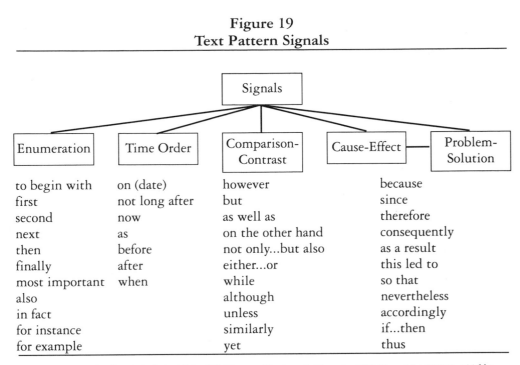

Enumeration	Time Order	Comparison-Contrast	Cause-Effect	Problem-Solution
to begin with	on (date)	however	because	
first	not long after	but	since	
second	now	as well as	therefore	
next	as	on the other hand	consequently	
then	before	not only...but also	as a result	
finally	after	either...or	this led to	
most important	when	while	so that	
also		although	nevertheless	
in fact		unless	accordingly	
for instance		similarly	if...then	
for example		yet	thus	

Pattern Guides can be used with students at virtually any level. For example, since we believe that the ability to discover cause-and-effect relationships should be developed at an early age, we have provided a cause/effect Pattern Guide for a primary-level textbook lesson on American history (Figure 20). Since younger students enjoy puzzles and manipulative activities, we've adapted the guide to include such activities.

After reading and discussing the relevant pages in the text, students can work in pairs or groups for the text structure lesson. As noted earlier, the teacher will want to model and thoroughly explain the text pattern to be studied, using everyday examples to show students the value of learning how factual information is put together.

Next, the teacher will need to develop cause-and-effect puzzle cards, using a different color for each category (e.g., red for causes, blue for effects). Laminating the cards will preserve them for repeated use. Page numbers can be written on the back so students know where to look for information in their books. The teacher can tell the groups to line up their puzzle parts with the causes on the left and the effects on the right. They should first read the information on an "effect" card and try to remember from their reading what the cause was; then they should refer back to the text for confirmation. The teacher can circulate around the groups to assist and assess progress. As a follow-up, we recommend asking the class to point out in their text the line or lines that support each of their matches. With this activity, the teacher helps students learn not just the information in the content area but actually how to read this type of material.

Figure 20
Pattern Guide
(social studies—primary level)

Cause/Effect Relationships

Cause	Effect	
More people came to America	Colonies were started	(p. 128)
England passed unfair laws	Colonists refused to obey the laws	(p. 129)
Colonists refused to obey laws	England sent soldiers to make colonists obey	(p. 129)
England sent soldiers to make colonists obey laws	Colonists went to war against England	(p. 129)
Colonists won the right to rule themselves	13 colonies became 13 states	(p. 129)
13 colonies became 13 states	New country called United States of America	(p. 129)

The Pattern Guide in Figure 21 was designed to accompany a middle-level history selection dealing with the Chinese government. The first part of the guide encourages students to focus on the main concepts before beginning the text structure activity. This type of activity is useful because it allows students to make their own choices about important concepts while helping them develop a cluster of knowledge about significant events in history.

The second part of the guide has students draw on the knowledge organized in the previous section to determine causes and effects. In this case the students complete a matching exercise, pairing the causes in the left-hand column with the effects in the right-hand column.

Figure 21
Pattern Guide
(history—middle level)

The Government of China

I. Directions: Read the section on "The Government of China" in your textbook (pages 274-77). As you read, write down three important points relating to each of the following topics.

    A. Chinese language
        1.
        2.
        3.
    B. Chinese religions
        1.
        2.
        3.
    C. Chinese communism
        1.
        2.
        3.

II. Directions: From the information above, we can begin to note a connection between various events in history. In this section, we will be examining the causes (*why* something happened) and effects (*what* happened) of historical events. Match each cause in the left-hand column with its effect from the right-hand column, putting the letter of the effect on the appropriate line.

Examples:

Cause	Effect
_B_ 1. The Chinese written language has thousands of symbols	(A) The Chinese could not share the advance of technology in the outside world.
_A_ 2. Mao Zedong instituted the Cultural Revolution.	(B) The Chinese government is actively working to simplify the language.

Exercise:

Cause	Effect
___ 3. The Chinese economic system is based on agricultural production.	(C) The communist government of China was originally modeled on the Soviet system.
___ 4. The eastern section of China has the most fertile land.	(D) Only 20% of the Chinese people live in the cities.
___ 5. The former Soviet Union was the first successful exporter of communism.	(E) Most Chinese people are farmers.
___ 6. The Chinese system allows active participation in only one political party.	(F) The Chinese government discourages religious beliefs.
___ 7. The Communist Party controls the activities of the Chinese government.	(G) 80% of the Chinese population is crowded into the eastern section of China.
___ 8. Religious practices are not sanctioned by communist governments.	(H) The head of the Communist Party is the leader of the country.
	(I) The Communist Party is the only legal political party in China.

Concept Guide

Concept Guides originated with Baker (1977), who maintains that within any pattern of organization certain concepts are more important than others and that students need help in distinguishing the more significant concepts from the less significant ones. Concept Guides are designed to help students organize information from text by categorizing subordinate information under the major concepts. The first part of the guide contains literal-level tasks and questions relating to the text selection. In the second part, students must place details or supporting ideas from the selection under the main concepts. A third section may involve a higher level of generalization in which students are required to find support from the selection for the main concepts.

Since all students can benefit from assistance in categorizing subordinate information under major concepts, these guides are appropriate for use with students at any grade level. The Concept Guide in Figure 22 was developed by an elementary teacher for use in a learning center by individuals or small groups. Rather than handing out a printed form, the teacher created sentence strips and word cards for the students to put together like a puzzle; presented this way, the strategy has much appeal for younger students.

To further enhance its utility, the lesson shown can easily be adapted for whole class use. In the first part, the students as a group place the statements under either the true or the false heading according to their existing prior knowledge. (A flannel board with sentence strips can be used here.) A lively discussion can ensue from this part of the activity. Although the statements themselves are at the literal level, the thinking that goes into determining placement is of a higher order. Next the students are instructed to read (or listen to) the text with the statements in mind. Afterwards, they go over their earlier choices and rearrange the statements under the correct headings, being certain to substantiate the reasons for their changes with information from the text.

Once satisfied with the arrangement of the concepts, the students can work in small groups to write or place each word from Part II of the guide under the correct heading. (As with Part I, this section can be done as a manipulative activity with word cards.) The students can refer back to their rearranged concept list in Part I or to their text for assistance. Then the class as a whole can discuss this categorization of terms.

Classroom Context:
Individual, small group, whole class

Subject:
Content areas

Level:
Primary, intermediate, middle, secondary

Figure 22
Concept Guide
(science—primary level)

I. Directions: Place each of these statements under either the "true" or the "false" heading.

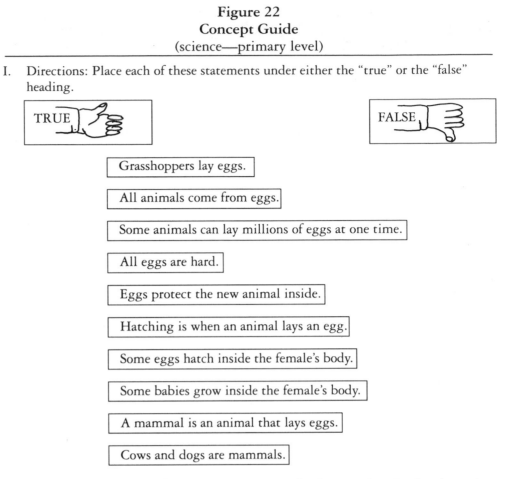

Grasshoppers lay eggs.

All animals come from eggs.

Some animals can lay millions of eggs at one time.

All eggs are hard.

Eggs protect the new animal inside.

Hatching is when an animal lays an egg.

Some eggs hatch inside the female's body.

Some babies grow inside the female's body.

A mammal is an animal that lays eggs.

Cows and dogs are mammals.

II. Directions: From the information given in your book, write [or place] each word or phrase from the word bank under the correct heading.

Word Bank

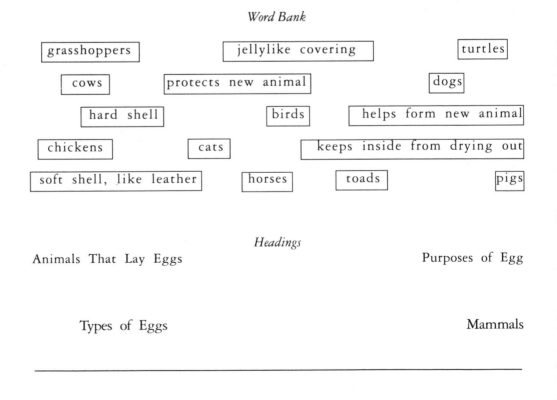

Headings

Animals That Lay Eggs   Purposes of Egg

Types of Eggs   Mammals

Figure 23 illustrates the Concept Guide with a middle-level history lesson on India. In Part I of the guide, students are instructed to read the text selection on their own, and then work in groups to determine which statements are supported in the passage. In Part II, the students write each checked statement on the line labeled "concept" and then add details from the text on the lines labeled "supporting information." A culminating activity for this lesson is the construction of a timeline, which further encourages students to use details in forming generalizations.

Figure 23
Concept Guide
(history—middle level)

Exploring the Non-Western World: India

I. Directions: Read the section in your textbook called "The India That Was" (pages 298-301) on your own. Then, in your groups, discuss each statement below and put a checkmark beside the ones that are specifically supported by the reading.

_____ 1. The first inhabitants of India were dark-skinned people determined to remain separate from others.

_____ 2. Hinduism, now the major religion of India, evolved over thousands of years from many religious beliefs.

_____ 3. An Indian prince named Siddhartha developed a new philosophy called Buddhism that de-emphasizes people's selfish desires.

_____ 4. Maurya rulers helped to spread Buddhism throughout India.

_____ 5. The expansion of technology during the Guptas' reign was the golden age of India.

_____ 6. The Muslim invasion of India contributed to a decline in Buddhism and a movement toward Islam.

_____ 7. The European invasion during the Age of Exploration introduced Christianity to India.

✓ 8. India experienced a progression of dominant religious and political systems.

_____ 9. Religious and political changes caused times of civil unrest and strife.

II. Directions: As a group, fill in the diagrams below by placing each statement you checked in Section I on the line labeled "Concept." Then find the details that support each concept and place them on the lines labeled "Supporting Information."

Figure 23
(continued)

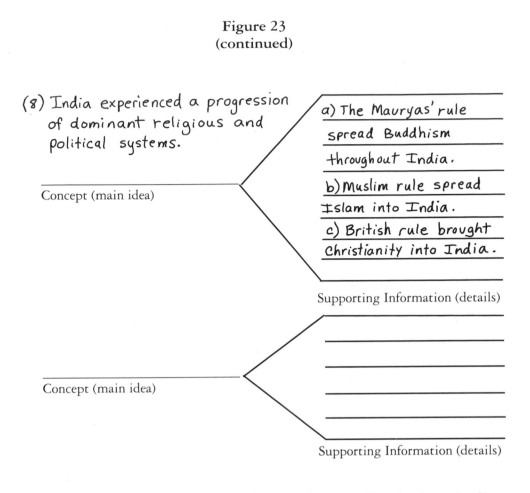

(8) India experienced a progression of dominant religious and political systems.

_____
Concept (main idea)

a) The Mauryas' rule spread Buddhism throughout India.

b) Muslim rule spread Islam into India.

c) British rule brought Christianity into India.

Supporting Information (details)

_____
Concept (main idea)

Supporting Information (details)

III.   Directions: In your group, use the information in Section II to develop a timeline to show the spread of different religions in India.

Analogical Study Guide

New information that is presented with analogies is often more vivid and easily understood. Taking advantage of this benefit, Bean, Singer, and Cowan (1985) developed the Analogical Study Guide to reinforce the learning of subject area material. These guides help learning by (1) making abstract concepts more imaginable, and (2) encouraging students to connect new information with everyday experiences.

Figure 24 demonstrates how the Analogical Study Guide can be used in a middle-level science classroom. The guide draws an analogy between components of the circulatory system and the more familiar elements of a road system. Hemoglobin, because it carries oxygen to the body, is compared to gasoline. White blood cells are compared to traffic cops because they fight disease and infection. To further enhance learning, the teacher can draw a road system that resembles the circulatory system, complete with the city (heart) and highways (veins).

Believing that analogies can and should be taught at all grade levels, we introduced the idea of the Analogical Study Guide to a creative primary-level teacher, who came up with the example in Figure 25. This guide begins with posters depicting how a plant and a person drinking through a straw receive nutrients. After reading the text selection with the students, the teacher refers to the first poster to identify plant parts and their functions and then turns to the poster of a person drinking through a straw to make the analogy. To actively involve the students, the teacher has included a demonstration of what happens to plants' nutrient-gathering capabilities under different conditions. This use of analogies can be very effective in building students' conceptual understanding of the topic under study.

Bean, Singer, and Cowan (1985) recommend three steps in developing an Analogical Study Guide. First, analyze the reading task to determine what concepts students should learn. Focus on essential information and eliminate the rest from further study. This will reinforce the notion that the textbook is a reference source from which the most important information can be gleaned.

The second step is to construct appropriate analogies. In their sample guide, Bean, Singer, and Cowan show how the 14 parts of a cell function similarly to the various parts of a factory. For example, the cell wall, whose main function is to provide support and protection, is related to factory walls. The cell membrane, which forms a boundary and serves as gatekeeper, is compared

Classroom Context:
Individual, small group, whole class

Subject:
Content areas

Level:
Primary, intermediate, middle, secondary

Figure 24
Analogical Study Guide
(science—middle level)

Circulatory System

Element of Circulatory System	Function	Similar Element of Road System
Red blood cells	Carry gases to and from the body's cells	Cars
Hemoglobin	Protein that carries oxygen to the body	Gasoline
Bone marrow	Makes red blood cells	Car factories and dealers
White blood cells	Fight diseases and infection	Traffic cops
Platelets	Produce blood clots that stop bleeding	Construction barriers
Arteries	Carry blood away from the heart	Highways
Veins	Carry blood to the heart	Numbered routes
Capillaries	Connect arteries to veins	Exit ramps
Heart	Muscular organ that pumps blood to the body	City

to factory security guards. The cell nucleus, which contains the organism's genetic coding, is analogous to the boss's office with a copy machine.

The third and crucial step in this process is to explain and demonstrate to students how the guide works. Be sure to illustrate how the analogies can be used as retrieval cues or mnemonic devices to help students recall information from text. The originators of this guide suggest that students be encouraged to develop their own analogies about a given topic to further enhance their learning. We believe that such a task could best be accomplished in small, heterogeneous groups in which students can brainstorm and test out their ideas on one another.

Bean, Singer, and Cowan caution that it is not always possible to develop analogies for the concept to be studied. But many topics, particularly those that introduce a lot of new vocabulary terms, lend themselves well to comparisons with more familiar objects.

Figure 25
Creating an Analogical Study Guide for Plants
(science—primary level)

Materials needed: Posters showing plant parts and a person drinking through a straw;
1 straw and cup (water inside) for each student; drawing paper; crayons.

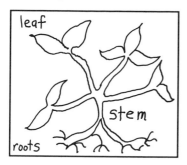

Procedure:

1. Read the relevant pages with your students. Write the words *leaf*, *stem*, and *root* on the board.

2. Refer to the poster on plant parts. Discuss it with the students and have them identify the parts, using the correct terminology.

3. Discuss and ask questions about the functions of different plant parts.
   a. root—gathers nutrients (food) from soil
   b. stem—carries food to leaves
   c. leaf—receives food in order to grow

4. Direct students' attention to the second poster. Ask them how a person drinking with a straw is like a growing plant.

5. Relate these concepts:
   a. root to cup (collects nutrients/food)
   b. stem to straw (carries food upward)
   c. leaf to person drinking (receives food)

6. Give each student a cup with water in it and a straw. Ask them to demonstrate how the leaves of a plant receive food from the soil just like a person receives liquid through a straw.

7. Students can also show what happens when leaves are pulled off a plant (they receive no food) by moving their mouths away from the straw.

8. What happens when the stem is broken off from the roots? Students can show this by taking the straw out of the water.

9. What happens when the soil has not been fertilized or watered? Have students pour out the water from the cup. There is no food for the straw (or the stem) to carry.

10. Have students draw the plant parts.

Content Guide

Karlin's (1964) Content Guide uses questions along with an information index to point out which content students should pay most attention to and where in the selection that content can be found. The index after each question directs students to the relevant information in the text by giving the page, column, and/or paragraph number. This allows students to focus on comprehending rather than on searching. Typical textbook questions provide no such clues for students; often they aren't even presented in sequential order. As a result, struggling readers must plod through the chapter to try and find the answers.

  The intermediate-level Content Guide in Figure 26 helps direct students' attention to the most significant information in a selection from their health text and points out where that information can be found. The questions on the Content Guide follow the order of the text so students won't have to spend time shuffling through the pages. Teachers can break down the reading into manageable segments by instructing students to read a question, then read the corresponding text page, and finally answer the question before moving on. This strategy keeps students from feeling overwhelmed by the vast amount of material encountered in a typical content area reading assignment.

  Teachers can design the Content Guide to work with students of different ability levels by making some questions optional. This helps to "slice the task" (Readence & Moore, 1980)—that is, it reduces the demands on less able readers by giving them fewer items to answer. As the example in the figure shows, the optional questions can have a less detailed information index, or even none at all, whereas the explicit pointers included with the mandatory questions provide extra assistance for those who need it.

  The Content Guide is one of the simplest study guides to develop and is also the most prototypical in its use of questions. As Karlin (1964) notes, though, its format can vary to include matching, sentence completion, and true/false items as well as questions.

  The items in the guide can be used for testing long-term recall or simply for aiding understanding during the reading process. A major objective of this guide is to develop "smaller" purposes for reading that are more focused than the overall purposes established at the prereading stage.

Classroom Context:
Individual, small group, whole class

Subject:
Content areas

Level:
Intermediate, middle, secondary

Figure 26
Content Guide
(health—intermediate level)

Microorganisms

As you read pages 166-74, answer the following questions:

1. What are the types of microorganisms? (p. 168)

2. Where are microorganisms found? (p. 168, paragraph 2, and p. 169, paragraph 1)

3. How do mircroorganisms cause communicable diseases? (p. 169, paragraph 5)

*4. Microorganisms grow well in garbage bins. Where are some other places they would grow well?

5. How can you protect yourself from harmful microorganisms when someone in your family is ill? (p. 170, paragraphs 3 & 4)

6. Why shouldn't you use pond water to clean a cut or scrape? (p. 171)

7. How do pests spread diseases? (p. 173)

*8. Why is it dangerous to refreeze meat once it has thawed?

*optional questions

Guide-O-Rama

Cunningham and Shablak (1975) developed the Selective Reading Guide-O-Rama to help students learn not only "what to look for, but specifically what to do with it" once they find it (p. 381). In this guide, the teacher begins by eliminating any sections of the chapter that do not help achieve the overall purpose for reading. Since less proficient readers tend to read either very laboriously or very rapidly, the Guide-O-Rama includes directives to govern students' reading speed. Such directives are designed to develop flexibility in reading rate and to teach students to skip over or read quickly through unimportant material.

Developing a successful Guide-O-Rama takes three steps. First, determine the overall purpose of the reading lesson by posing the question, "What do I want the students to learn from this selection?" Second, select those portions of the text that will help students achieve the overall lesson purpose and eliminate from consideration the irrelevant portions. The underlying concept here is that textbooks should be used as resource books from which important information can be gleaned. It is not necessary that students read and respond to every word, but rather that they come away with a practical understanding of the most significant concepts. The third step is to review the sections that remain, determine what the reader must do to achieve the lesson purpose, and develop task statements accordingly.

The Guide-O-Rama excerpt displayed in Figure 27 helps students determine how long to spend on different portions of a health passage and indicates what information deserves the most attention. An icon next to each task statement cues students at the outset to adjust their reading speed to coordinate with the demands of the reading task. (If you use such icons, be sure to explain their meanings to the students.) Notice how for paragraphs 1 and 2 on page 95 students are instructed to read quickly, focusing on understanding what a calorie is and what it does. The last item tells students to skim to find out what is needed for maintaining a desirable weight, while the item before requires a more thorough reading and organizing of the material presented.

Classroom Context:
Individual, small group, whole class

Subject:
Content areas

Level:
Intermediate, middle, secondary

Figure 27
Guide-O-Rama
(health—middle level)

How Much Should You Eat?

Page 95, title
    Read the title. Briefly answer the question posed by the title.

Page 95, paragraph 1
    Paragraph 1 introduces the material. Read it quickly.

Page 95, paragraph 2
    Paragraph 2 describes what *calories* are and what they do. Be sure you understand calories before you go on.

Page 95, paragraphs 3, 4, and 5

    As you read paragraphs 3, 4, and 5 under "Choosing the Right Amount for You," compare the number of calories (or food) needed for girls and boys; for large persons and small persons; and for active and inactive persons. (Making a chart may be helpful.)

Page 96, paragraph 1
    Skim through the section "Controlling Your Weight" to determine what is needed for maintaining a desirable weight.

Reading Road Map

As with the Guide-O-Rama, one assumption underlying the Reading Road Map (Wood, 1988) is that poor comprehenders tend to read all material at the same rate—either very quickly or very slowly and deliberately. The Reading Road Map guides students through the content by helping them adjust their reading rate to correspond with the importance of the concepts encountered. A typical Reading Road Map comprises missions (interspersed questions and activities), road signs (reading rate indicators), and location signs (headings and page or paragraph numbers). Students can choose or be assigned a "traveling companion" for their journey through the text.

Because this approach is novel, it tends to capture the attention of students who are difficult to motivate. It can be modified and used at any grade level, although in the secondary years, it is probably most appropriate for the remedial or resource room setting.

The Reading Road Map shown in Figure 28 guides intermediate-level students through a chapter on arthropods. Students engage in a variety of activities along the way, including retelling, recalling, outlining, and comparing. The traveling companions can take turns reading portions of the text and deciding on the most logical answers. The teacher may intervene at various points during the journey to provide additional explanations or to request comments from the students.

The last "mission" in this guide is for students to think back on the trip to recall whatever they can about the four types of arthropods described in the chapter. This type of mental review aids long-term recall. Teachers can use the study guide to teach this strategy and then instruct students to apply the mental review process independently with later reading assignments.

It's important to thoroughly explain the purpose of the Reading Road Map. Parallels can be drawn between the "textbook journey" and an actual trip to another location. In reading, as with travel, it is much less confusing to look ahead, plan your course, and know where you are going before you get there. An introduction such as the following should pique interest:

> We have discussed how difficult it can be to read and thoroughly understand all of the new information in our textbooks. So, instead of just reading the next chapter, we are going on a tour together—a tour of the world of arthropods. We'll stop along the way to take a closer look at some of the things we find. Oh, and I have made a map for us to use. We'll skim it first to get an idea of what we will see before we actually make the journey. Then we'll be off!

Classroom Context:
Individual, small group, whole class

Subject:
Content areas

Level:
Primary, intermediate, middle, secondary

Figure 28
Reading Road Map
(science—intermediate level)

Chapter 13: Arthropods

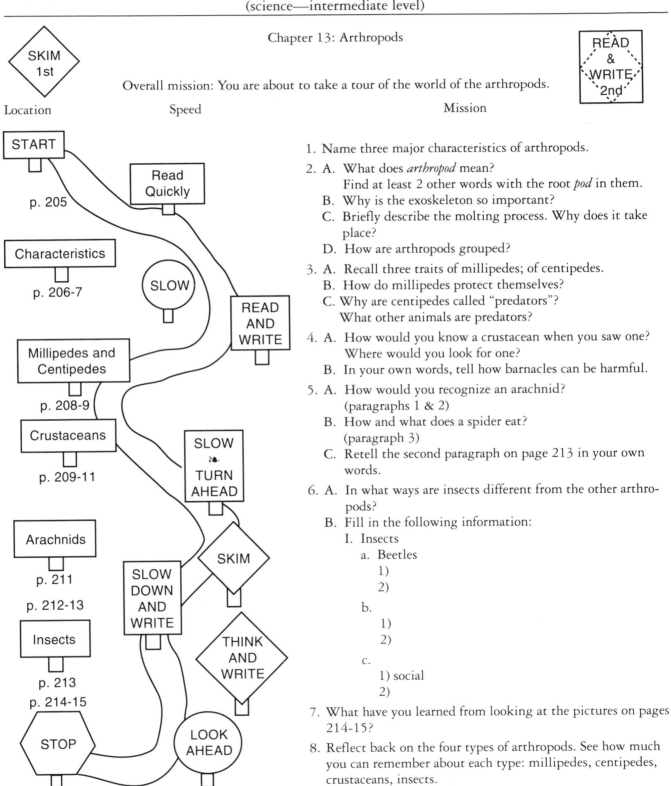

Overall mission: You are about to take a tour of the world of the arthropods.

Location   Speed   Mission

SKIM 1st

READ & WRITE 2nd

START
p. 205

Read Quickly

Characteristics
p. 206-7

SLOW

READ AND WRITE

Millipedes and Centipedes
p. 208-9

Crustaceans
p. 209-11

SLOW & TURN AHEAD

Arachnids
p. 211
p. 212-13

SKIM

SLOW DOWN AND WRITE

Insects
p. 213
p. 214-15

THINK AND WRITE

STOP

LOOK AHEAD

1. Name three major characteristics of arthropods.
2. A. What does *arthropod* mean?
      Find at least 2 other words with the root *pod* in them.
   B. Why is the exoskeleton so important?
   C. Briefly describe the molting process. Why does it take place?
   D. How are arthropods grouped?
3. A. Recall three traits of millipedes; of centipedes.
   B. How do millipedes protect themselves?
   C. Why are centipedes called "predators"?
      What other animals are predators?
4. A. How would you know a crustacean when you saw one?
      Where would you look for one?
   B. In your own words, tell how barnacles can be harmful.
5. A. How would you recognize an arachnid?
      (paragraphs 1 & 2)
   B. How and what does a spider eat?
      (paragraph 3)
   C. Retell the second paragraph on page 213 in your own words.
6. A. In what ways are insects different from the other arthropods?
   B. Fill in the following information:
      I. Insects
         a. Beetles
            1)
            2)
         b.
            1)
            2)
         c.
            1) social
            2)
7. What have you learned from looking at the pictures on pages 214-15?
8. Reflect back on the four types of arthropods. See how much you can remember about each type: millipedes, centipedes, crustaceans, insects.

From Wood, K.D. (1988). Guiding students through informational text. *The Reading Teacher. 41*(9), 912-920. Reprinted by permission of the International Reading Association.

Glossing

Although the use of marginal notes, or glossing, dates back to medieval times (Richgels & Hansen, 1984), Otto et al. (1981) are generally credited with demonstrating how this strategy can be used to improve students' understanding of text. Glossing directs students' attention as they read; teachers can use it to focus on the process of reading (skills and strategies), the content of what is to be read (facts, information, concepts), or both.

Because standard glossing requires that notations be made in the text itself, teachers may feel it is inappropriate, especially since most schools forbid marking in textbooks. If this is the case, the teacher may choose to use a modified version wherein notations are printed on a sort of bookmark and then aligned with the text (this is similar to the Process Guide, discussed later). Glossing can also be undertaken on chart paper or the chalkboard in the modeling phase of a lesson to help students learn to apply specific strategies or concepts to their reading material.

The example shown in Figure 29 was developed for a secondary-level English class in which students were learning how to interpret the metaphorical language of poetry. The teacher started out by glossing a sample poem, repro-

Classroom Context:
Individual, small group, whole class

Subject:
Literature, content areas

Level:
Primary, intermediate, middle, secondary

▼ ▼ ▼

Figure 29
Glossing
(English—secondary level)

On the Grasshopper and Cricket

John Keats ———— What is the poetry of the Earth?

The [poetry of earth] is never dead:
    When all the birds are faint with the hot sun,   What is the voice? Are there
    And hide in cooling trees, [a voice will run]   more than one?
[From hedge to hedge about the new-mown [mead:]]   [meadow]
[That is the grasshopper's—he takes the lead   [Indicates constant move-
    In summer luxury,—he has never done]   ment of nature through
    With his delights; for when tired out with fun   the seasons]
He rests at ease beneath some pleasant weed.   Why is the grasshopper the
The poetry of earth is ceasing never: summer poet?
    On a lone winter evening, when the frost
    Has (wrought) a silence, from the stove there shrills   [made]
[The Cricket's song, in warmth increasing ever,]   Why is the cricket the winter
    And seems to one in drowsiness half lost,   poet?
    The Grasshopper's among some grassy hills.   What is the difference
    between the grasshopper's song
    and the cricket's song?

ducing it, and distributing it to the class for further explanation. (Note that this poem is in the public domain, so reproducing it is not a copyright infringement. Teachers need to take copyright issues into account before reproducing any published material.) The glosses focused both on terminology and on broader meaning. Next the teacher displayed a different poem on a transparency and guided the class in working through the poem and discussing its implications. During this exercise, the teacher recorded the students' contributions and interpretations. Afterwards the teacher distributed a copy of a third poem and had students work in pairs to gloss their interpretations.

A similar process can be used with content area material. Providing a glossed science passage, for example, can help students learn to use context to interpret new vocabulary, understand typographical aids such as bold print and italics, or draw inferences from the text, among other skills.

To develop a gloss selection, Richgels and Hansen (1984) suggest three general guidelines. The first is to examine the text to determine which skills and strategies are needed to maximize comprehension. Successful readers point to four strategies as the most useful in reading content area texts: establishing a purpose for reading, relating the content to prior knowledge, organizing the incoming information, and monitoring one's own comprehension (Otto et al., 1981).

Gloss notations can be developed to help students engage in these strategies as they read. Some sample notations follow:

Establishing a purpose

- As you read, note several characteristics of each of the explorers discussed.
- After reading this selection, you should be able to explain how light is reflected on objects.

Using prior knowledge

- What are some other words you know with the prefix *micro?*
- Indicate what comes to your mind when you think about Japan.

Organizing new information

- Compare and contrast the three main characters in the story.
- Three subheadings tell you the three functions of the cardiovascular system. List and briefly describe each one.

Monitoring comprehension

- Answer the following questions:
  1. The process of photosynthesis takes place when _____ _____.

  2. Plants need photosynthesis in order to _____ _____.

- How certain are you of your answers?

  #1   sure   not sure

  #2   sure   not sure

  Go back to the section on photosynthesis to check the answers of which you are uncertain.

Another guideline for glossing is to be aware of students' level of understanding. Students who have difficulty understanding content area vocabulary will need notations that explain meanings in straightforward terms. Textbook authors sometimes erroneously assume that readers possess the knowledge necessary to understand a concept; when that happens, the teacher can use a gloss notation to provide the extra explanation needed.

Finally, be aware of the physical and personal realities of the classroom environment. Make certain that the gloss notations are brief and used only when necessary to meet lesson objectives. Otherwise, struggling comprehenders will have another abundance of print to wade through in attempting to understand their reading.

Process Guide

The Process Guide (Karlin, 1964) is designed to help students identify which skills are necessary to master specific content. Unlike a typical study guide, it is not duplicated on regular-size paper. Instead, it is printed on a strip of paper resembling a bookmark, which students line up with the text. According to Karlin, a Process Guide can cover several skill areas, including recognizing text structure, drawing inferences, selecting important information, evaluating content, and figuring out context clues.

The Process Guide is similar to glossing, except that it never requires marking up the actual text, which makes it a preferred choice for many teachers. The Process Guide can be used at any grade level and in any content area. It is particularly useful for studying poetry in language arts because it directs students' attention to features like similes, metaphors, contrasts, and alliteration. In other subjects, it can be used to point out certain key words and their definitions or to signal students to make predictions, draw conclusions, or ponder an idea. It can also be used to point out the main idea of a paragraph, the text structure or pattern used, when information is implied rather than directly stated, and other aspects of writing.

In Figure 30 we show how the Process Guide can be used with younger students who are just becoming acquainted with the density of concepts and complex sentence structure of content area material. Bookmark-like cards or rectangles of paper should be prepared in advance to accompany pages in the text requiring special attention. Students can keep these bookmarks for reference later on.

Process Guides should focus on the most significant information from each passage. To do that, they can ask questions, present various tasks to be undertaken, or point out particular areas for students to focus on. Their flexible purpose allows them to be used in a variety of ways. Students can keep the bookmarks in their texts to refresh their memories of certain passages or gather together the bookmarks for studying longer segments. Working with a partner, they can also use the key concepts on the cards to trigger more elaborate associations from their reading and class discussions. Once the teacher feels comfortable that the students are beginning to understand how to select key concepts, he or she can instruct the students to develop their own Process Guides, either independently or in pairs.

Classroom Context:
Individual, small group, whole class

Subject:
Math, literature, content areas

Level:
Primary, intermediate, middle, secondary

Figure 30
Process Guide
(history—primary level)

George Washington and Washington, D.C.

Americans chose

————————— as

the first

————————.

Name 4 things you
learned about the
capital of the United States.
1) —————————
2) —————————
3) —————————
4) —————————

The land for the capital
was in
————— and —————

It was named

————————— for

—————————.

Americans planned a new government. They chose their own leaders and made their own laws. Americans chose George Washington as their leader again. He became the first president of the United States.

At first Americans could not agree on a place for the capital of the new country. A capital is the city where government leaders work. The country's capital was moved from place to place. Then leaders decided to ask President Washington to choose a place.

Washington picked a place on the Potomac River. The land was part of two states, Maryland and Virginia. The states gave up the land, and it was named Washington, D.C., after the first President.

Text excerpted from Kahney, M., 1988, p. 130.

Figure 31 shows how the Process Guide can be used in an intermediate-level science lesson on energy chains. Once students read the initial paragraph their first task is to construct a diagram illustrating the relationship described. The second item requires them to relate the new information to what they've learned previously. Finally, students are instructed to focus on the cause and effect relationship described in the second paragraph, thus helping them understand the text structure as well as the important information it contains.

Figure 31
Process Guide
(science—intermediate level)

Energy Chains

Draw a diagram to depict the energy chain in a flashlight. Compare and contrast this chain with other energy chains we have studied. Note the cause and effect relationship here.	For example, think about a flashlight. You can trace the energy chain in a flashlight. When the flashlight is on, the chemicals in the batteries react. Chemical energy changes to electric energy in the batteries. The electric energy flows into the bulb. The bulb gives off light energy. You begin with chemical energy and end with light energy. Energy is transferred and changed in an energy chain. As energy moves along the chain, the energy receivers become energy sources. Heat energy changes into mechanical energy in a gasoline engine. Heat causes the gases in a chamber to expand. When the gases expand, a piston is forced down and a crank turns. Heat can do work by changing into mechanical energy to move an object.

From Sund, R.B. et al., 1985, p. 254. Reprinted by permission of the Glencoe Division of the Macmillan/McGraw-Hill School Publishing Company.

Guidelines
for Classroom Use

In this section we present a number of suggestions to help teachers develop and implement the types of study guides we've described. As with any instructional strategy, you'll need to adapt your approach to take into account the students' abilities, the demands of the text, and your lesson objectives. However, these general guidelines should help in any situation.

Include a review of the content.   Frequent review of information learned improves long-term understanding and retention (Good & Grouws, 1979). As shown in the examples presented earlier, the culminating activity of a study guide should involve a mental and written review of the major concepts, events, or people discussed in the text. Ask students to associate the new information with their prior knowledge and to recall all they can while the information is still readily accessible.

Be creative in designing the guides.   The more creative the guide is in appearance and content, the more likely it is that students will want to read the assigned text. A guide on the cardiovascular system, for example, may take the shape of a heart with questions or activities marking significant locations. Guide questions and activities should likewise be designed to stimulate creative thinking.

Group and pair students.   The Interactive Reading Guide is designed specifically to capitalize on the many advantages of cooperative learning, but all reading guides should have some element of student-to-student and student-to-teacher interaction. Such collaboration not only improves achievement but also greatly enhances relationships among students (Johnson & Johnson, 1985).

Have students skim before beginning.   Skimming the guide and the text before beginning should become automatic for students after the initial instruction and modeling. This survey step helps students solidify their purpose for reading and allows them to see where they are going before they get there.

Explain and model.   Ample research attests to the value of modeling skills and strategies before assigning independent practice (Berliner & Rosenshine, 1977; Duffy & McIntyre, 1981). It is essential that the teacher thoroughly explain the purpose of the reading guides and "walk and talk" students through the assignment. This helps students gain a metacognitive understanding of why such guides can help them learn.

Circulate and monitor.   The most effective teachers continually circulate and monitor class assignments (Evertson et al., 1984; Kounin, 1970). This level of involvement in the lesson allows the teacher to assist individuals or groups and to determine who may need further encouragement.

Follow with a discussion.   Study guides require teacher direction to be effective. Their value diminishes when students are told merely to turn in their assignment when finished. Follow-up discussions of students' guide responses are essential with each lesson to increase interest, learning, and later recall.

Use study guides judiciously.   Study guides should not be designed for every chapter or selection. As with any strategy, their novelty would soon wear off and their utility diminish. Use of guides should be limited to portions of the text that may be difficult for students to follow or that are particularly suitable for such treatment.

Avoid assigning grades.   Study guides are adjunct aids developed to assist students with reading classroom material. Therefore, they should not be graded in the competitive sense, particularly since the finished guides are often the result of a group effort. Group members should be given either a "complete" or an "incomplete," if any grade at all.

Encourage strategic reading.   Strategic readers read purposefully and with direction, and they know what to do when something fails to make sense. In short, they know what strategies to use and when to use them (Paris, Lipson, & Wixson, 1983). Study guides are a means of making students aware of the range of strategies necessary for successful comprehension. It is essential to explain how these strategies apply to other contexts (both within and outside of the classroom) and how they can be employed independently when no guide is available.

A Final Note

This monograph provides a comprehensive review of study guides to help teachers decide when and how to use these comprehension aids. Rather than relying on one or two well-known guides for all purposes, teachers can select from a variety of guides to align their purposes for teaching a particular lesson with their desired outcomes.

Study guides are useful classroom tools because teachers cannot always provide one-on-one assistance to their students. Guides can act as personal tutors by focusing students' attention on important information and thus reducing the amount of print encountered at any one time. They can be valuable tools for enhancing instruction at any grade level and in any content field.

References

Andre, T., Mueller, C., Womack, S., Smid, K., & Tuttle, M. (1980). Adjunct or application questions facilitate later application—or do they? *Journal of Educational Psychology, 70,* 796-803.

Armbruster, B. (1984). The problem of "inconsiderate text." In G.G. Duffy, L.R. Roehler, & J. Mason (Eds.), *Comprehension instruction: Perspectives and suggestions.* White Plains, NY: Longman.

Baker, R.L. (1977). The effects of inferential organizers on learning and retention, content knowledge, and term relationships in ninth grade social studies. In H.L. Herber & R.T. Vacca (Eds.), *Research in reading in the content areas: The third report.* Syracuse, NY: Syracuse University Reading and Language Arts Center.

Bean, T.W., Singer, H., & Cowan, S. (1985, December). Analogical study guides: Improving comprehension in science. *Journal of Reading, 29,* 246-250.

Berget, E. (1977). The use of organizational pattern guides, structural overviews, and visual summaries in guiding social studies reading. In H.L. Herber & R.T. Vacca (Eds.), *Research in reading in the content areas: The third report.* Syracuse, NY: Syracuse University Reading and Language Arts Center.

Berliner, D.C., & Rosenshine, B.V. (1977). The acquisition of knowledge in the classroom. In R.C. Anderson, R.J. Spiro, & W. Montague (Eds.), *Schooling and the acquisition of knowledge.* Hillsdale, NJ: Erlbaum.

Cunningham, D., & Shablak, S.L. (1975, February). Selective Reading Guide-O-Rama: The content teacher's best friend. *Journal of Reading. 18.* 380-382.

Davey, B. (1986). Using textbook activity guides to help students learn from textbooks. *Journal of Reading. 29.* 489-494.

Distad, H.W. (1927, January). A study of the reading performance of pupils under different conditions on different types of materials. *Journal of Educational Psychology. 18.* 247-258.

Duffelmeyer, F.A., Baum, D.D., & Merkley, D.J. (1987, November). Maximizing reader-text confrontation with an Extended Anticipation Guide. *Journal of Reading. 31,* 146-150.

Duffy, G.G,. & McIntyre, L. (1981). A naturalistic study of teacher assistance behavior in primary classrooms. *Elementary School Journal. 83,* 15-23.

Durrell, D.D. (1956). *Improving reading instruction.* Orlando, FL: Harcourt Brace Jovanovich.

Earle, R.A. (1969). Use of the structured overview in mathematics classes. In H.L. Herber & P.L. Sanders (Eds.), *Research in reading in the content areas: First year report.* Syracuse, NY: Syracuse University Reading and Language Arts Center.

Estes, T.H. (1969). Use of prepared guide material and small group discussion in reading ninth grade social studies assignments. In H.L. Herber & P.L. Sanders (Eds.), *Research in reading in the content areas: First year report.* Syracuse, NY: Syracuse University Reading and Language Arts Center.

Evertson, C., Emmer, E.T., Clements, B.S., Sanford, J.P., & Worsham, M.E. (1984). *Classroom management for elementary teachers.* Englewood Cliffs, NJ: Prentice Hall.

Faw, H.W., & Waller, T.G. (1976). Mathemagenic behaviors and efficiency in learning from prose materials: Review, critique, and recommendations. *Review of Educational Research, 46,* 691-720.

Frase, L.T. (1968a). Effect of question location, pacing, and mode upon retention of prose material. *Journal of Educational Psychology, 59,* 244-249.

Frase, L.T. (1968b). Questions as aids to reading: Some research and theory. *American Education Research Journal, 5,* 319-332.

Good, T., & Grouws, D. (1979). The Missouri mathematics effectiveness project: An experimental study in fourth grade classrooms. *Journal of Educational Psychology, 71,* 355-362.

Herber, H.L. (1970). *Teaching reading in the content areas.* Englewood Cliffs, NJ: Prentice Hall.

Hershberger, W. (1964). Self-evaluational responding and typographical cueing: Techniques for programming self-instructional reading materials. *Journal of Educational Psychology, 55,* 288-296.

Johnson, R.T, & Johnson, D.W. (1985, July/August). Student-student interaction: Ignored but powerful. *Journal of Teacher Education, 36,* 22-26.

Kahney, M. (1988). *Neighborhoods and communities.* Glenview, IL: Scott, Foresman.

Karlin, R. (1964). *Teaching reading in high school.* New York: Bobbs-Merrill.

Kounin, J. (1970). *Discipline and group management in classrooms.* Orlando, FL: Holt, Rinehart & Winston.

Lapp, D., & Flood, J. (1991). *Teaching reading to every child* (3rd ed.). New York: Macmillan.

MacDonald-Ross, M. (1978). Language in texts: The design of curricular materials. In L.S. Shulman (Ed.), *Review of research in education.* Itasca, IL: Peacock.

Maxon, G.A. (1979). An investigation of the relative effect of questions and declarative statements as guides to reading comprehension for seventh grade students. In H.L. Herber & J.D. Riley (Eds.), *Research in reading in the content areas: The fourth report.* Syracuse, NY: Syracuse University Reading and Language Arts Center.

Nichols, J.N. (1983). Using prediction to increase content area interest and understanding. *Journal of Reading, 27,* 225-228.

Otto, W., White, S., Richgels, D., Hansen, R., & Morrison, B. (1981). *A technique for improving the understanding of expository text: Gloss and examples* (Theoretical Paper No. 96). Madison, WI: Wisconsin Center for Education Research.

Paris, S.G., Lipson, M.Y., & Wixson, K.K. (1983). Becoming a strategic reader. *Contemporary Educational Psychology, 8,* 293-316.

Pauk, W. (1974). *How to study in college.* Boston, MA: Houghton Mifflin.

Raphael, T. (1984, January). Teaching learners about sources of information for answering comprehension questions. *Journal of Reading, 27,* 303-311.

Readence, J.E., Bean, T., & Baldwin, R.S. (1981). *Content area reading: An integrated approach.* Dubuque, IA: Kendall/Hunt.

Readence, J.E., & Moore, D. (1980). Differentiating text assignments in content areas: Slicing the task. *Reading Horizons, 20,* 112-117.

Richgels, D.J., & Hansen, R. (1984, January). Gloss: Helping students apply both skills and strategies in reading content texts. *Journal of Reading, 27,* 312-317.

Rickards, J.P. (1979). Adjunct postquestions in text: A critical review of methods and processes. *Review of Educational Research, 49*, 181-196.

Rickards, J.P., & Denner, P.R. (1978). Inserted questions as aids to reading text. *Instructional Science, 7*, 313-346.

Rickards, J.P., & DiVesta, F.J. (1974). Type and frequency of questions in processing textual materials. *Journal of Educational Psychology, 66*, 354-362.

Riley, J.D. (1979). The effects of reading guides and a directed reading method on word problem comprehension, problem solving ability, and attitude towards mathematics. In H.L. Herber & J.D. Riley (Eds.), *Research in reading in the content areas: The fourth report.* Syracuse, NY: Syracuse University Reading and Language Arts Center.

Rothkopf, E.Z. (1972). Learning from written instructive materials: An explanation of the control of inspection behavior by test-like events. *American Educational Research Journal, 3*, 241-249.

Singer, H., & Donlan, D. (1980). *Reading and learning from text.* Boston, MA: Little, Brown.

Singer H., & Donlan, D. (1989). *Reading and learning from text* (2nd ed.). Hillsdale, NJ: Erlbaum.

Sund, R.B., Adams, D.K., Hackett, J.K., & Moyer, R.H. (1985). *Accent on science.* Columbus, OH: Merrill.

Tierney, R.J., & Cunningham, J.W. (1984). Research on teaching reading comprehension. In P.D. Pearson (Ed.), *Handbook of reading research.* White Plains, NY: Longman.

Vacca, R.T. (1981). *Content area reading.* Boston, MA: Little, Brown.

Vacca, R.T., & Vacca, J.L. (1989). *Content area reading* (3rd ed.). Glenview, IL: Scott, Foresman.

Washburne, J.N. (1929, May). The use of questions in social science material. *Journal of Educational Psychology, 20*, 321-359.

Wood, K.D. (1986, Summer). The effects of interspersing questions in text: Evidence for slicing the task. *Reading Research and Instruction, 25*, 295-307.

Wood, K.D. (1987). Helping students comprehend their textbooks. *Middle School Journal, 18*(2), 20-21.

Wood, K.D. (1988). Guiding students through informational text. *The Reading Teacher, 41*(9), 912-920.

Wood, K.D. (1990a). Collaborative strategies for improving students' conceptual understanding of mathematics. Paper presented at the Macmillan Symposium on Mathematics and Science, Santa Fe, NM.

Wood, K.D. (1990b). Meaningful approaches to vocabulary development. *Middle School Journal, 21*, 22-24.

Wood, K.D. (in press). The study guide: A strategy review. *The Reading Professor.*

Wood, K.D., & Mateja, J.A. (1983, February). Adapting secondary level strategies for use in elementary classrooms. *The Reading Teacher, 36*(6), 492-496.